WORDS FOR THE WIND

The Collected Verse of

THEODORE
ROETHKE

Roethke, Theodore, 1908-1963.

WORDS

FOR

THE WIND

DOUBLEDAY & COMPANY, INC., GARDEN CITY, N.Y.

Thanks are due to the following periodicals in whose pages some of these poems have appeared: Poetry: A Magazine of Verse, The Atlantic Monthly, The Sewanee Review, The Kenyon Review, Partisan Review, The Hudson Review, Landmarks and Voyages (The Poetry Book Society Limited), The Times Literary Supplement, The Listener, The Observer, The London Magazine, The New Statesman and Nation, Botteghe Oscure, Encounter, Poetry-London-New York, Harper's Bazaar, The New Republic, and Poems in Folio. The following poems appeared originally in The New Yorker: *Vernal Sentiment*, *Night Journey*, *Forcing House*, *Frau Bauman*, *Frau Schmidt and Frau Schwartze*, *The Dream*, *The Voice*, *Snake*, *They Sing*, *The Small*, *I'm Here*, *A Walk in Late Summer*, *The Cantankerous One* (*The Surly One*), and *The Renewal*. *The Swan* was especially written for Poets and the Past, published by Andre Emmerich Gallery.

CONTENTS

PART TWO NEW POEMS

Lighter Pieces and Poems for Children
AN INTERLUDE

Love Poems 141

Voices and Creatures 169

PART ONE

THE
WAKING

from OPEN HOUSE

1941

OPEN HOUSE

My secrets cry aloud.
I have no need for tongue.
My heart keeps open house,
My doors are widely swung.
An epic of the eyes
My love, with no disguise.

My truths are all foreknown,
This anguish self-revealed.
I'm naked to the bone,
With nakedness my shield.
Myself is what I wear:
I keep the spirit spare.

The anger will endure,
The deed will speak the truth
In language strict and pure.
I stop the lying mouth:
Rage warps my clearest cry
To witless agony.

DEATH PIECE

Invention sleeps within a skull
No longer quick with light,
The hive that hummed in every cell
Is now sealed honey-tight.

His thought is tied, the curving prow
Of motion moored to rock;
And minutes burst upon a brow
Insentient to shock.

TO MY SISTER

O my sister remember the stars the tears the trains
The woods in spring the leaves the scented lanes
Recall the gradual dark the snow's unmeasured fall
The naked fields the cloud's immaculate folds
Recount each childhood pleasure: the skies of azure
The pageantry of wings the eye's bright treasure.

Keep faith with present joys refuse to choose
Defer the vice of flesh the irrevocable choice
Cherish the eyes the proud incredible poise
Walk boldly my sister but do not deign to give
Remain secure from pain preserve thy hate thy heart.

INTERLUDE

The element of air was out of hand.
The rush of wind ripped off the tender leaves
And flung them in confusion on the land.
We waited for the first rain in the eaves.

The chaos grew as hour by hour the light
Decreased beneath an undivided sky.
Our pupils widened with unnatural night,
But still the road and dusty field kept dry.

The rain stayed in its cloud; full dark came near;
The wind lay motionless in the long grass.
The veins within our hands betrayed our fear.
What we had hoped for had not come to pass.

PRAYER

If I must of my Senses lose,
I pray Thee, Lord, that I may choose
Which of the Five I shall retain
Before oblivion clouds the brain.
My Tongue is generations dead,
My Nose defiles a comely head;
For hearkening to carnal evils
My Ears have been the very devil's.
And some have held the Eye to be
The instrument of lechery,
More furtive than the Hand in low
And vicious venery— Not so!
Its rape is gentle, never more
Violent than a metaphor.
In truth, the Eye's the abettor of
The holiest platonic love:
Lip, Breast and Thigh cannot possess
So singular a blessedness.
Therefore, O Lord, let me preserve
The Sense that does so fitly serve,
Take Tongue and Ear—all else I have—
Let Light attend me to the grave!

THE ADAMANT

Thought does not crush to stone.
The great sledge drops in vain.
Truth never is undone;
Its shafts remain.

The teeth of knitted gears
Turn slowly through the night,
But the true substance bears
The hammer's weight.

Compression cannot break
A center so congealed;
The tool can chip no flake:
The core lies sealed.

MID-COUNTRY BLOW

All night and all day the wind roared in the trees,
Until I could think there were waves rolling high as my bedroom
   floor;
When I stood at the window, an elm bough swept to my knees;
The blue spruce lashed like a surf at the door.

The second dawn I would not have believed:
The oak stood with each leaf stiff as a bell.
When I looked at the altered scene, my eye was undeceived,
But my ear still kept the sound of the sea like a shell.

THE HERON

The heron stands in water where the swamp
Has deepened to the blackness of a pool,
Or balances with one leg on a hump
Of marsh grass heaped above a musk-rat hole.

He walks the shallow with an antic grace.
The great feet break the ridges of the sand,
The long eye notes the minnow's hiding place.
His beak is quicker than a human hand.

He jerks a frog across his bony lip,
Then points his heavy bill above the wood.
The wide wings flap but once to lift him up.
A single ripple starts from where he stood.

THE BAT

By day the bat is cousin to the mouse.
He likes the attic of an aging house.

His fingers make a hat about his head.
His pulse beat is so slow we think him dead.

He loops in crazy figures half the night
Among the trees that face the corner light.

But when he brushes up against a screen,
We are afraid of what our eyes have seen:

For something is amiss or out of place
When mice with wings can wear a human face.

NO BIRD

Now here is peace for one who knew
The secret heart of sound.
The ear so delicate and true
Is pressed to noiseless ground.

Slow swings the breeze above her head,
The grasses whitely stir;
But in this forest of the dead
No bird awakens her.

Long live the weeds that overwhelm
My narrow vegetable realm!
The bitter rock, the barren soil
That force the son of man to toil;
All things unholy, marred by curse,
The ugly of the universe.
The rough, the wicked, and the wild
That keep the spirit undefiled.
With these I match my little wit
And earn the right to stand or sit,
Hope, love, create, or drink and die:
These shape the creature that is I.

EPIDERMAL MACABRE

Indelicate is he who loathes
The aspect of his fleshy clothes,—
The flying fabric stitched on bone,
The vesture of the skeleton,
The garment neither fur nor hair,
The cloak of evil and despair,
The veil long violated by
Caresses of the hand and eye.
Yet such is my unseemliness:
I hate my epidermal dress,
The savage blood's obscenity,
The rags of my anatomy,
And willingly would I dispense
With false accouterments of sense,
To sleep immodestly, a most
Incarnadine and carnal ghost.

ON THE ROAD TO WOODLAWN

I miss the polished brass, the powerful black horses,
The drivers creaking the seats of the baroque hearses,
The high-piled floral offerings with sentimental verses,
The carriages reeking with varnish and stale perfume.

I miss the pallbearers momentously taking their places,
The undertaker's obsequious grimaces,
The craned necks, the mourners' anonymous faces,
—And the eyes, still vivid, looking up from a sunken room.

ACADEMIC

The stethoscope tells what everyone fears:
You're likely to go on living for years,
With a nurse-maid waddle and a shop-girl simper,
And the style of your prose growing limper and limper.

VERNAL SENTIMENT

Though the crocuses poke up their heads in the usual places,
The frog scum appear on the pond with the same froth of green,
And boys moon at girls with last year's fatuous faces,
I never am bored, however familiar the scene.

When from under the barn the cat brings a similar litter,—
Two yellow and black, and one that looks in between,—
Though it all happened before, I cannot grow bitter:
I rejoice in the spring, as though no spring ever had been.

SALE

For sale: by order of the remaining heirs
Who ran up and down the big center stairs
The what-not, the settee, the Chippendale chairs
—And an attic of horrors, a closet of fears.

The furniture polished and polished so grand,
A stable and paddock, some fox-hunting land,
The summer house shaped like a village band stand
—And grandfather's sinister hovering hand.

The antimacassar for the sofa in red,
The Bechstein piano, the four-poster bed,
The library used as a card room instead
—And some watery eyes in a Copley head.

The dining room carpet dyed brighter than blood,
The table where everyone ate as he should,
The sideboard beside which a tall footman stood
—And a fume of decay that clings fast to the wood.

The hand-painted wall-paper, finer than skin,
The room that the children had never been in,
All the rings and the relics encrusted with sin
—And the taint in a blood that was running too thin.

NIGHT JOURNEY

Now as the train bears west,
Its rhythm rocks the earth,
And from my Pullman berth
I stare into the night
While others take their rest.
Bridges of iron lace,
A suddenness of trees,
A lap of mountain mist
All cross my line of sight,
Then a bleak wasted place,
And a lake below my knees.
Full on my neck I feel
The straining at a curve;
My muscles move with steel,
I wake in every nerve.
I watch a beacon swing
From dark to blazing bright;
We thunder through ravines
And gullies washed with light.
Beyond the mountain pass
Mist deepens on the pane;
We rush into a rain
That rattles double glass.
Wheels shake the roadbed stone,
The pistons jerk and shove,
I stay up half the night
To see the land I love.

from THE LOST SON

AND OTHER POEMS

1948

I

CUTTINGS

Sticks-in-a-drowse droop over sugary loam,
Their intricate stem-fur dries;
But still the delicate slips keep coaxing up water;
The small cells bulge;

One nub of growth
Nudges a sand-crumb loose,
Pokes through a musty sheath
Its pale tendrilous horn.

CUTTINGS
later

This urge, wrestle, resurrection of dry sticks,
Cut stems struggling to put down feet,
What saint strained so much,
Rose on such lopped limbs to a new life?

I can hear, underground, that sucking and sobbing,
In my veins, in my bones I feel it,—
The small waters seeping upward,
The tight grains parting at last.
When sprouts break out,
Slippery as fish,
I quail, lean to beginnings, sheath-wet.

ROOT CELLAR

Nothing would sleep in that cellar, dank as a ditch,
Bulbs broke out of boxes hunting for chinks in the dark,
Shoots dangled and drooped,
Lolling obscenely from mildewed crates,
Hung down long yellow evil necks, like tropical snakes.
And what a congress of stinks!—
Roots ripe as old bait,
Pulpy stems, rank, silo-rich,
Leaf-mold, manure, lime, piled against slippery planks.
Nothing would give up life:
Even the dirt kept breathing a small breath.

FORCING HOUSE

Vines tougher than wrists
And rubbery shoots,
Scums, mildews, smuts along stems,
Great cannas or delicate cyclamen tips,—
All pulse with the knocking pipes
That drip and sweat,
Sweat and drip,
Swelling the roots with steam and stench,
Shooting up lime and dung and ground bones,—
Fifty summers in motion at once,
As the live heat billows from pipes and pots.

WEED PULLER

Under the concrete benches,
Hacking at black hairy roots,—
Those lewd monkey-tails hanging from drainholes,—
Digging into the soft rubble underneath,
Webs and weeds,
Grubs and snails and sharp sticks,
Or yanking tough fern-shapes,
Coiled green and thick, like dripping smilax,
Tugging all day at perverse life:
The indignity of it!—
With everything blooming above me,
Lilies, pale-pink cyclamen, roses,
Whole fields lovely and inviolate,—
Me down in that fetor of weeds,
Crawling on all fours,
Alive, in a slippery grave.

ORCHIDS

They lean over the path,
Adder-mouthed,
Swaying close to the face,
Coming out, soft and deceptive,
Limp and damp, delicate as a young bird's tongue;
Their fluttery fledgling lips
Move slowly,
Drawing in the warm air.

And at night,
The faint moon falling through whitewashed glass,
The heat going down
So their musky smell comes even stronger,
Drifting down from their mossy cradles:
So many devouring infants!
Soft luminescent fingers,
Lips neither dead nor alive,
Loose ghostly mouths
Breathing.

MOSS-GATHERING

To loosen with all ten fingers held wide and limber
And lift up a patch, dark-green, the kind for lining cemetery baskets,
Thick and cushiony, like an old-fashioned doormat,
The crumbling small hollow sticks on the underside mixed with roots,
And wintergreen berries and leaves still stuck to the top,—
That was moss-gathering.
But something always went out of me when I dug loose those carpets
Of green, or plunged to my elbows in the spongy yellowish moss of
  the marshes:
And afterwards I always felt mean, jogging back over the logging road,
As if I had broken the natural order of things in that swampland;
Disturbed some rhythm, old and of vast importance,
By pulling off flesh from the living planet;
As if I had committed, against the whole scheme of life, a desecration.

Where were the greenhouses going,
Lunging into the lashing
Wind driving water
So far down the river
All the faucets stopped?—
So we drained the manure-machine
For the steam plant,
Pumping the stale mixture
Into the rusty boilers,
Watching the pressure gauge
Waver over to red,
As the seams hissed
And the live steam
Drove to the far
End of the rose-house,
Where the worst wind was,
Creaking the cypress window-frames,
Cracking so much thin glass
We stayed all night,
Stuffing the holes with burlap;
But she rode it out,
That old rose-house,
She hove into the teeth of it,
The core and pith of that ugly storm,
Ploughing with her stiff prow,
Bucking into the wind-waves
That broke over the whole of her,
Flailing her sides with spray,
Flinging long strings of wet across the roof-top,
Finally veering, wearing themselves out, merely
Whistling thinly under the wind-vents;

She sailed until the calm morning,
Carrying her full cargo of roses.

OLD FLORIST

That hump of a man bunching chrysanthemums
Or pinching-back asters, or planting azaleas,
Tamping and stamping dirt into pots,—
How he could flick and pick
Rotten leaves or yellowy petals,
Or scoop out a weed close to flourishing roots,
Or make the dust buzz with a light spray,
Or drown a bug in one spit of tobacco juice,
Or fan life into wilted sweet-peas with his hat,
Or stand all night watering roses, his feet blue in rubber boots.

FRAU BAUMAN, FRAU SCHMIDT, AND FRAU SCHWARTZE

Gone the three ancient ladies
Who creaked on the greenhouse ladders,
Reaching up white strings
To wind, to wind
The sweet-pea tendrils, the smilax,
Nasturtiums, the climbing
Roses, to straighten
Carnations, red
Chrysanthemums; the stiff
Stems, jointed like corn,
They tied and tucked,—
These nurses of nobody else.
Quicker than birds, they dipped
Up and sifted the dirt;
They sprinkled and shook;
They stood astride pipes,
Their skirts billowing out wide into tents,
Their hands twinkling with wet;
Like witches they flew along rows
Keeping creation at ease;
With a tendril for needle
They sewed up the air with a stem;
They teased out the seed that the cold kept asleep,—
All the coils, loops, and whorls.
They trellised the sun; they plotted for more than themselves.

I remember how they picked me up, a spindly kid,
Pinching and poking my thin ribs
Till I lay in their laps, laughing,
Weak as a whiffet;

Now, when I'm alone and cold in my bed,
They still hover over me,
These ancient leathery crones,
With their bandannas stiffened with sweat,
And their thorn-bitten wrists,
And their snuff-laden breath blowing lightly over me in my first sleep.

TRANSPLANTING

Watching hands transplanting,
Turning and tamping,
Lifting the young plants with two fingers,
Sifting in a palm-full of fresh loam,—
One swift movement,—
Then plumping in the bunched roots,
A single twist of the thumbs, a tamping and turning,
All in one,
Quick on the wooden bench,
A shaking down, while the stem stays straight,
Once, twice, and a faint third thump,—
Into the flat-box it goes,
Ready for the long days under the sloped glass:

The sun warming the fine loam,
The young horns winding and unwinding,
Creaking their thin spines,
The underleaves, the smallest buds
Breaking into nakedness,
The blossoms extending
Out into the sweet air,
The whole flower extending outward,
Stretching and reaching.

CHILD ON TOP OF A GREENHOUSE

The wind billowing out the seat of my britches,
My feet crackling splinters of glass and dried putty,
The half-grown chrysanthemums staring up like accusers,
Up through the streaked glass, flashing with sunlight,
A few white clouds all rushing eastward,
A line of elms plunging and tossing like horses,
And everyone, everyone pointing up and shouting!

FLOWER DUMP

Cannas shiny as slag,
Slug-soft stems,
Whole beds of bloom pitched on a pile,
Carnations, verbenas, cosmos,
Molds, weeds, dead leaves,
Turned-over roots
With bleached veins
Twined like fine hair,
Each clump in the shape of a pot;
Everything limp
But one tulip on top,
One swaggering head
Over the dying, the newly dead.

CARNATIONS

Pale blossoms, each balanced on a single jointed stem,
The leaves curled back in elaborate Corinthian scrolls;
And the air cool, as if drifting down from wet hemlocks,
Or rising out of ferns not far from water,
A crisp hyacinthine coolness,
Like that clear autumnal weather of eternity,
The windless perpetual morning above a September cloud.

2

MY PAPA'S WALTZ

The whiskey on your breath
Could make a small boy dizzy;
But I hung on like death:
Such waltzing was not easy.

We romped until the pans
Slid from the kitchen shelf;
My mother's countenance
Could not unfrown itself.

The hand that held my wrist
Was battered on one knuckle;
At every step you missed
My right ear scraped a buckle.

You beat time on my head
With a palm caked hard by dirt,
Then waltzed me off to bed
Still clinging to your shirt.

PICKLE BELT

The fruit rolled by all day.
They prayed the cogs would creep;
They thought about Saturday pay,
And Sunday sleep.

Whatever he smelled was good:
The fruit and flesh smells mixed.
There beside him she stood,—
And he, perplexed;

He, in his shrunken britches,
Eyes rimmed with pickle dust,
Prickling with all the itches
Of sixteen-year-old lust.

DOLOR

I have known the inexorable sadness of pencils,
Neat in their boxes, dolor of pad and paper-weight,
All the misery of manilla folders and mucilage,
Desolation in immaculate public places,
Lonely reception room, lavatory, switchboard,
The unalterable pathos of basin and pitcher,
Ritual of multigraph, paper-clip, comma,
Endless duplication of lives and objects.
And I have seen dust from the walls of institutions,
Finer than flour, alive, more dangerous than silica,
Sift, almost invisible, through long afternoons of tedium,
Dropping a fine film on nails and delicate eyebrows,
Glazing the pale hair, the duplicate gray standard faces.

THE RETURN

I circled on leather paws
In the darkening corridor,
Crouched closer to the floor,
Then bristled like a dog.

As I turned for a backward look,
The muscles in one thigh
Sagged like a frightened lip.

A cold key let me in
That self-infected lair;
And I lay down with my life,
With the rags and rotting clothes,
With a stump of scraggy fang
Bared for a hunter's boot.

LAST WORDS

Solace of kisses and cookies and cabbage,
That fine fuming stink of particular kettles,
Muttony tears falling on figured linoleum,
Frigidaires snoring the sleep of plenty,
The psyche writhing and squirming in heavy woolen,—
O worm of duty! O spiral knowledge!

Kiss me, kiss me quick, mistress of lost wisdom,
Come out of a cloud, angel with several faces,
Bring me my hat, my umbrella and rubbers,
Enshroud me with Light! O Whirling! O Terrible Love!

NIGHT CROW

When I saw that clumsy crow
Flap from a wasted tree,
A shape in the mind rose up:
Over the gulfs of dream
Flew a tremendous bird
Further and further away
Into a moonless black,
Deep in the brain, far back.

THE MINIMAL

I study the lives on a leaf: the little
Sleepers, numb nudgers in cold dimensions,
Beetles in caves, newts, stone-deaf fishes,
Lice tethered to long limp subterranean weeds,
Squirmers in bogs,
And bacterial creepers
Wriggling through wounds
Like elvers in ponds,
Their wan mouths kissing the warm sutures,
Cleaning and caressing,
Creeping and healing.

THE CYCLE

Dark water, underground,
Beneath the rock and clay,
Beneath the roots of trees,
Moved into common day,
Rose from a mossy mound
In mist that sun could seize.

The fine rain coiled in a cloud
Turned by revolving air
Far from that colder source
Where elements cohere
Dense in the central stone.
The air grew loose and loud.

Then, with diminished force,
The full rain fell straight down,
Tunneled with lapsing sound
Under even the rock-shut ground,
Under a river's source,
Under primeval stone.

from PRAISE TO THE END

1951

I

WHERE KNOCK IS OPEN WIDE

1

A kitten can
Bite with his feet;
Papa and Mamma
Have more teeth.

Sit and play
Under the rocker
Until the cows
All have puppies.

His ears haven't time.
Sing me a sleep-song, please.
A real hurt is soft.

Once upon a tree
I came across a time,
It wasn't even as
A ghoulie in a dream.

There was a mooly man
Who had a rubber hat
And funnier than that,—
He kept it in a can.

What's the time, papa-seed?
Everything has been twice.
My father is a fish.

2

I sing a small sing,
My uncle's away,
He's gone for always,
I don't care either.

I know who's got him,
They'll jump on his belly,
He won't be an angel,
I don't care either.

I know her noise.
Her neck has kittens.
I'll make a hole for her.
In the fire.

Winkie will yellow I sang.
Her eyes went kissing away
It was and it wasn't her there
I sang I sang all day.

3

I know it's an owl. He's making it darker.
Eat where you're at. I'm not a mouse.
Some stones are still warm.
I like soft paws.
Maybe I'm lost,
Or asleep.

A worm has a mouth.
Who keeps me last?
Fish me out.
Please.

God, give me a near. I hear flowers.
A ghost can't whistle.
I know! I know!
Hello happy hands.

4

We went by the river.
Water birds went ching. Went ching.
Stepped in wet. Over stones.
One, his nose had a frog,
But he slipped out.

I was sad for a fish.
Don't hit him on the boat, I said.
Look at him puff. He's trying to talk.
Papa threw him back.

Bullheads have whiskers.
And they bite.

    He watered the roses.
    His thumb had a rainbow.
    The stems said, Thank you.
    Dark came early.

That was before. I fell! I fell!
The worm has moved away.
My tears are tired.

Nowhere is out. I saw the cold.
Went to visit the wind. Where the birds die.
How high is have?

I'll be a bite. You be a wink.
Sing the snake to sleep.

5

Kisses come back,
I said to Papa;
He was all whitey bones
And skin like paper.

God's somewhere else,
I said to Mamma.
The evening came
A long long time.

I'm somebody else now.
Don't tell my hands.
Have I come to always? Not yet.
One father is enough.

Maybe God has a house.
But not here.

I NEED, I NEED

1

A deep dish. Lumps in it.
I can't taste my mother.
Hoo. I know the spoon.
Sit in my mouth.

A sneeze can't sleep.
Diddle we care
Couldly.

Went down cellar,
Talked to a faucet;
The drippy water
Had nothing to say.

Whisper me over,
Why don't you, begonia,
There's no alas
Where I live.

Scratched the wind with a stick.
The leaves liked it.
Do the dead bite?
Mamma, she's a sad fat.

A dove said dove all day.
A hat is a house.
I hid in his.

2

Even steven all is less:
I haven't time for sugar,
Put your finger in your face,
And there will be a booger.

    A one is a two is
    I know what you is:
    You're not very nice,—
    So touch my toes twice.

I know you are my nemesis
So bibble where the pebble is.
The Trouble is with No and Yes
As you can see I guess I guess.

    I wish I was a pifflebob
    I wish I was a funny
    I wish I had ten thousand hats,
    And made a lot of money.

Open a hole and see the sky:
A duck knows something
You and I don't.
Tomorrow is Friday.

    Not you I need.
    Go play with your nose.
    Stay in the sun,
    Snake-eyes.

3

Stop the larks. Can I have my heart back?
Today I saw a beard in a cloud.
The ground cried my name:
Good-bye for being wrong.
Love helps the sun.
But not enough.

4

When you plant, spit in the pot.
A pick likes to hit ice.
Hooray for me and the mice!—
The oats are all right.

Hear me, soft ears and roundy stones!
It's a dear life I can touch.
Who's ready for pink and frisk?
My hoe eats like a goat.

    Her feet said yes.
    It was all hay.
    I said to the gate,
    Who else knows
    What water does?
    Dew ate the fire.

I know another fire.
Has roots.

1

Bees and lilies there were,
Bees and lilies there were,
Either to other,—
Which would you rather?
Bees and lilies were there.

The green grasses,—would they?
The green grasses?—
She asked her skin
To let me in:
The far leaves were for it.

Forever is easy, she said.
How many angels do you know?—
And over by Algy's
Something came by me,
It wasn't a goose,
It wasn't a poodle.

Everything's closer. Is this a cage?
The chill's gone from the moon.
Only the woods are alive.
I can't marry the dirt.

I'm a biscuit. I'm melted already.
The white weather hates me.
Why is how I like it.
I can't catch a bush.

2

The herrings are awake.
What's all the singing between?—
Is it with whispers and kissing?—
I've listened into the least waves.
The grass says what the wind says:
Begin with the rock;
End with water.

    When I stand, I'm almost a tree.
    Leaves, do you like me any?
    A swan needs a pond.
    The worm and the rose
    Both love
    Rain.

3

O small bird wakening,
Light as a hand among blossoms,
Hardly any old angels are around any more.
The air's quiet under the small leaves.
The dust, the long dust, stays.
The spiders sail into summer.
It's time to begin!
To begin!

1

Believe me, knot of gristle, I bleed like a tree;
I dream of nothing but boards;
I could love a duck.

Such music in a skin!
A bird sings in the bush of your bones.
Tufty, the water's loose.
Bring me a finger. This dirt's lonesome for grass.
Are the rats dancing? The cats are.
And you, cat after great milk and vasty fishes,
A moon loosened from a stag's eye,
Twiced me nicely,—
In the green of my sleep,
In the green.

2

Mother of blue and the many changes of hay,
This tail hates a flat path.
I've let my nose out;
I could melt down a stone,—
How is it with the long birds?
May I look too, loved eye?
It's a wink beyond the world.
In the slow rain, who's afraid?
We're king and queen of the right ground.
I'll risk the winter for you.

You tree beginning to know,
You whisper of kidneys,

We'll swinge the instant!—
With jots and jogs and cinders on the floor:
The sea will be there, the great squashy shadows,
Biting themselves perhaps;
The shrillest frogs;
And the ghost of some great howl
Dead in a wall.
In the high-noon of thighs,
In the springtime of stones,
We'll stretch with the great stems.
We'll be at the business of what might be
Looking toward what we are.

3

You child with a beast's heart,
Make me a bird or a bear!
I've played with the fishes
Among the unwrinkling ferns
In the wake of a ship of wind;
But now the instant ages,
And my thought hunts another body.
I'm sad with the little owls.

4

Touch and arouse. Suck and sob. Curse and mourn.
It's a cold scrape in a low place.
The dead crow dries on a pole.
Shapes in the shade
Watch.

The mouth asks. The hand takes.
These wings are from the wrong nest.
Who stands in a hole
Never spills.

I hear the clap of an old wind.
The cold knows when to come.
What beats in me
I still bear.

The deep stream remembers:
Once I was a pond.
What slides away
Provides.

SENSIBILITY! O LA!

1

I'm the serpent of somebody else.
See! She's sleeping like a lake:
Glory to seize, I say.

> In the fair night of some dim brain,
> Thou wert marmorean-born.
> I name thee: wench of things,
> A true zephyr-haunted woodie.
> The sea's unequal lengths announced thy birth
> From a shell harder than horn.
> Thy soft albino gaze
> Spoke to my spirit.

It's queer enough here, perhaps.
Some rare new tedium's taking shape:
I smell the jumps ahead.
Can a cat milk a hen?

2

A whisper of what,
You round dog?—
Is the wasp tender?
John-of-the-thumb's jumping;
Commodities, here we come!

> A shape comes to stay:
> The long flesh.
> I know the way out of a laugh;
> I'm a twig to touch,
> Pleased as a knife.

3

You all-of-a-sudden gods,
There's a ghost loose in the long grass!
My sweetheart's still in her cave.
I've waked the wrong wind:
I'm alone with my ribs;
The lake washes its stones.
You've seen me, prince of stinks,
Naked and entire.
Exalted? Yes,—
By the lifting of the tail of a neighbor's cat,
Or that old harpy secreting toads in her portmanteau.
Mamma! Put on your dark hood;
It's a long way to somewhere else.
The shade says: love the sun.
I have.
La, la,
The light turns.
The moon still abides.
I hear you, alien of the moon.
Is the sun under my arm?
My sleep deceives me.
Has the dark a door?
I'm somewhere else,—
I insist!
I am.

O LULL ME, LULL ME

1

One sigh stretches heaven.
In this, the diocese of mice,
Who's bishop of breathing?

How still she keeps herself.
Blessed be torpor.
Not all animals
Move about.

Tell me, great lords of sting,
Is it time to think?
When I say things fond,
I hear singing.
O my love's light as a duck
On a moon-forgotten wave!

The sea has many streets;
The beach rises with the waves.
I know my own bones:
This doxie doesn't do.

2

The air, the air provides.
Light fattens the rock.
Let's play before we forget!

A wish! A wish!
O lovely chink, O white
Way to another grace!—

I see my heart in the seed;
I breathe into a dream,
And the ground cries.
I'm crazed and graceless,
A winter-leaping frog.

Soothe me, great groans of underneath,
I'm still waiting for a foot.
The poke of the wind's close,
But I can't go leaping alone.
For you, my pond,
Rocking with small fish,
I'm an otter with only one nose:
I'm all ready to whistle;
I'm more than when I was born;
I could say hello to things;
I could talk to a snail;
I see what sings!
What sings!

2

THE LOST SON

1 *The Flight*

At Woodlawn I heard the dead cry:
I was lulled by the slamming of iron,
A slow drip over stones,
Toads brooding in wells.
All the leaves stuck out their tongues;
I shook the softening chalk of my bones,
Saying,
Snail, snail, glister me forward,
Bird, soft-sigh me home.
Worm, be with me.
This is my hard time.

Fished in an old wound,
The soft pond of repose;
Nothing nibbled my line,
Not even the minnows came.

Sat in an empty house
Watching shadows crawl,
Scratching.
There was one fly.

Voice, come out of the silence.
Say something.
Appear in the form of a spider
Or a moth beating the curtain.

Tell me:
Which is the way I take;
Out of what door do I go,
Where and to whom?

Dark hollows said, lee to the wind,
The moon said, back of an eel,
The salt said, look by the sea,
Your tears are not enough praise,
You will find no comfort here,
In the kingdom of bang and blab.

Running lightly over spongy ground,
Past the pasture of flat stones,
The three elms,
The sheep strewn on a field,
Over a rickety bridge
Toward the quick-water, wrinkling and rippling.

Hunting along the river,
Down among the rubbish, the bug-riddled foliage,
By the muddy pond-edge, by the bog-holes,
By the shrunken lake, hunting, in the heat of summer.

The shape of a rat?
It's bigger than that.
It's less than a leg
And more than a nose,
Just under the water
It usually goes.

Is it soft like a mouse?
Can it wrinkle its nose?

Could it come in the house
On the tips of its toes?

Take the skin of a cat
And the back of an eel,
Then roll them in grease,—
That's the way it would feel.

It's sleek as an otter
With wide webby toes
Just under the water
It usually goes.

2 The Pit

Where do the roots go?
  Look down under the leaves.
Who put the moss there?
  These stones have been here too long.
Who stunned the dirt into noise?
  Ask the mole, he knows.
I feel the slime of a wet nest.
  Beware Mother Mildew.
Nibble again, fish nerves.

3 The Gibber

At the wood's mouth,
By the cave's door,
I listened to something
I had heard before.

Dogs of the groin
Barked and howled,

The sun was against me,
The moon would not have me.

The weeds whined,
The snakes cried,
The cows and briars
Said to me: Die.

What a small song. What slow clouds. What dark water.
Hath the rain a father? All the caves are ice. Only the snow's here.
I'm cold. I'm cold all over. Rub me in father and mother.
Fear was my father, Father Fear.
His look drained the stones.

> What gliding shape
> Beckoning through halls,
> Stood poised on the stair,
> Fell dreamily down?

> From the mouths of jugs
> Perched on many shelves,
> I saw substance flowing
> That cold morning.

> Like a slither of eels
> That watery cheek
> As my own tongue kissed
> My lips awake.

Is this the storm's heart? The ground is unstilling itself.
My veins are running nowhere. Do the bones cast out their fire?
Is the seed leaving the old bed? These buds are live as birds.
Where, where are the tears of the world?
Let the kisses resound, flat like a butcher's palm;

82

Let the gestures freeze; our doom is already decided.
All the windows are burning! What's left of my life?
I want the old rage, the lash of primordial milk!
Good-bye, good-bye, old stones, the time-order is going,
I have married my hands to perpetual agitation,
I run, I run to the whistle of money.

Money money money
Water water water

How cool the grass is.
Has the bird left?
The stalk still sways.
Has the worm a shadow?
What do the clouds say?

These sweeps of light undo me.
Look, look, the ditch is running white!
I've more veins than a tree!
Kiss me, ashes, I'm falling through a dark swirl.

4 *The Return*

The way to the boiler was dark,
Dark all the way,
Over slippery cinders
Through the long greenhouse.

The roses kept breathing in the dark.
They had many mouths to breathe with.
My knees made little winds underneath
Where the weeds slept.

There was always a single light
Swinging by the fire-pit,
Where the fireman pulled out roses,
The big roses, the big bloody clinkers.

Once I stayed all night.
The light in the morning came slowly over the white
Snow.
There were many kinds of cool
Air.
Then came steam.

Pipe-knock.

Scurry of warm over small plants.
Ordnung! Ordnung!
Papa is coming!

A fine haze moved off the leaves;
Frost melted on far panes;
The rose, the chrysanthemum turned toward the light.
Even the hushed forms, the bent yellowy weeds
Moved in a slow up-sway.

5 (*It was beginning winter.*)

It was beginning winter,
An in-between time,
The landscape still partly brown:
The bones of weeds kept swinging in the wind,
Above the blue snow.

It was beginning winter.
The light moved slowly over the frozen field,

Over the dry seed-crowns,
The beautiful surviving bones
Swinging in the wind.

Light traveled over the field;
Stayed.
The weeds stopped swinging.
The mind moved, not alone,
Through the clear air, in the silence.

Was it light?
Was it light within?
Was it light within light?
Stillness becoming alive,
Yet still?

A lively understandable spirit
Once entertained you.
It will come again.
Be still.
Wait.

THE LONG ALLEY

1

A river glides out of the grass. A river or a serpent.
A fish floats belly upward,
Sliding through the white current,
Slowly turning,
Slowly.

The dark flows on itself. A dead mouth sings under an old tree.
The ear hears only in low places.
Remember an old sound.
Remember
Water.

This slag runs slow. What bleeds when metal breaks?
Flesh, you offend this metal. How long need the bones mourn?
Are those horns on top of the hill? Yesterday has a long look.

Loo, loo, said the sulphurous water,
There's no filth on a plateau of cinders.
This smoke's from the glory of God.

Can you name it? I can't name it.
Let's not hurry. The dead don't hurry.
Who else breathes here? What does the grave say?
My gates are all caves.

2

The fiend's far away. Lord, what do you require?
The soul resides in the horse barn.
Believe me, there's no one else, kitten-limp sister.

86

Kiss the trough, swine-on-Friday.
Come to me, milk-nose. I need a loan of the quick.
   There's no joy in soft bones.
For whom were you made, sweetness I cannot touch?
   Look what the larks do.
Luminous one, shall we meet on the bosom of God?
   Return the gaze of a pond.

3

Stay close. Must I kill something else?
Can feathers eat me? There's no clue in the silt.
This wind gives me scales. Have mercy, gristle:
It's my last waltz with an old itch.

    A waiting ghost warms up the dead
    Until they creak their knees:
    So up and away and what do we do
    But barley-break and squeeze.

    Tricksy comes and tricksy goes
    Bold in fear therefore;
    The hay hops in the horse's mouth,
    The chin jumps to the nose.

    Rich me cherries a fondling's kiss,
    The summer bumps of ha:
    Hand me a feather, I'll fan you warm,
    I'm happy with my paws.

Gilliflower ha,
Gilliflower ho,
My love's locked in

The old silo.
She cries to the hen,
She waves to the goose,
But they don't come
To let her loose.

    If we detach
    The head of a match
    What do we do
    To the cat's wish?
    Do we rout the fish?
    Will the goat's mouth
    Have the last laugh?

4

That was a close knock. See what the will wants.
This air could flesh a dead stick. Sweet Jesus, make me sweat.
Are the flowers here? The birds are.
Shall I call the flowers?

    Come littlest, come tenderest,
    Come whispering over the small waters,
    Reach me rose, sweet one, still moist in the loam,
    Come, come out of the shade, the cool ways,
    The long alleys of string and stem;
    Bend down, small breathers, creepers and winders;
    Lean from the tiers and benches,
    Cyclamen dripping and lilies.
    What fish-ways you have, littlest flowers,
    Swaying over the walks, in the watery air,
    Drowsing in soft light, petals pulsing.

Light airs! Light airs! A pierce of angels!
The leaves, the leaves become me!
The tendrils have me!

5

Bricks flake before my face. Master of water, that's trees away.
Reach me a peach, fondling, the hills are there.
Nuts are money: wherefore and what else?
Send down a rush of air, O torrential,
Make the sea flash in the dust.

Call off the dogs, my paws are gone.
This wind brings many fish;
The lakes will be happy:
Give me my hands:
I'll take the fire.

A FIELD OF LIGHT

Came to lakes; came to dead water,
Ponds with moss and leaves floating,
Planks sunk in the sand.

A log turned at the touch of a foot;
A long weed floated upward;
An eye tilted.

    Small winds made
    A chilly noise;
    The softest cove
    Cried for sound.

    Reached for a grape
    And the leaves changed;
    A stone's shape
    Became a clam.

    A fine rain fell
    On fat leaves;
    I was there alone
    In a watery drowse.

2

Angel within me, I asked,
Did I ever curse the sun?
Speak and abide.

Under, under the sheaves,
Under the blackened leaves,
Behind the green viscid trellis,
In the deep grass at the edge of a field,
Along the low ground dry only in August,—

Was it dust I was kissing?
A sigh came far.
Alone, I kissed the skin of a stone;
Marrow-soft, danced in the sand.

3

The dirt left my hand, visitor.
I could feel the mare's nose.
A path went walking.
The sun glittered on a small rapids.
Some morning thing came, beating its wings.
The great elm filled with birds.

Listen, love,
The fat lark sang in the field;
I touched the ground, the ground warmed by the killdeer,
The salt laughed and the stones;
The ferns had their ways, and the pulsing lizards,
And the new plants, still awkward in their soil,
The lovely diminutives.

I could watch! I could watch!
I saw the separateness of all things!
My heart lifted up with the great grasses;
The weeds believed me, and the nesting birds.
There were clouds making a rout of shapes crossing a windbreak of
   cedars,

And a bee shaking drops from a rain-soaked honeysuckle.
The worms were delighted as wrens.
And I walked, I walked through the light air;
I moved with the morning.

THE SHAPE OF THE FIRE

1

What's this? A dish for fat lips.
Who says? A nameless stranger.
Is he a bird or a tree? Not everyone can tell.

Water recedes to the crying of spiders.
An old scow bumps over black rocks.
A cracked pod calls.

Mother me out of here. What more will the bones allow?
Will the sea give the wind suck? A toad folds into a stone.
These flowers are all fangs. Comfort me, fury.
Wake me, witch, we'll do the dance of rotten sticks.

Shale loosens. Marl reaches into the field. Small birds pass over water.
Spirit, come near. This is only the edge of whiteness.
I can't laugh at a procession of dogs.

In the hour of ripeness, the tree is barren.
The she-bear mopes under the hill.
Mother, mother, stir from your cave of sorrow.

A low mouth laps water. Weeds, weeds, how I love you.
The arbor is cooler. Farewell, farewell, fond worm.
The warm comes without sound.

2

Where's the eye?
The eye's in the sty.
The ear's not here

Beneath the hair.
When I took off my clothes
To find a nose,
There was only one shoe
For the waltz of To,
The pinch of Where.

Time for the flat-headed man. I recognize that listener,
Him with the platitudes and rubber doughnuts,
Melting at the knees, a varicose horror.
Hello, hello. My nerves knew you, dear boy.
Have you come to unhinge my shadow?
Last night I slept in the pits of a tongue.
The silver fish ran in and out of my special bindings;
I grew tired of the ritual of names and the assistant keeper of the
    mollusks:
Up over a viaduct I came, to the snakes and sticks of another winter,
A two-legged dog hunting a new horizon of howls.
The wind sharpened itself on a rock;
A voice sang:

Pleasure on ground
Has no sound,
Easily maddens
The uneasy man.

Who, careless, slips
In coiling ooze
Is trapped to the lips,
Leaves more than shoes;

Must pull off clothes
To jerk like a frog

On belly and nose
From the sucking bog.

My meat eats me. Who waits at the gate?
Mother of quartz, your words writhe into my ear.
Renew the light, lewd whisper.

3

The wasp waits.
    The edge cannot eat the center.
The grape glistens.
    The path tells little to the serpent.
An eye comes out of the wave.
    The journey from flesh is longest.
A rose sways least.
    The redeemer comes a dark way.

4

Morning-fair, follow me further back
Into that minnowy world of weeds and ditches,
When the herons floated high over the white houses,
And the little crabs slipped into silvery craters.
When the sun for me glinted the sides of a sand grain,
And my intent stretched over the buds at their first trembling.

That air and shine: and the flicker's loud summer call:
The bearded boards in the stream and the all of apples;
The glad hen on the hill; and the trellis humming.
Death was not. I lived in a simple drowse:
Hands and hair moved through a dream of wakening blossoms.
Rain sweetened the cave and the dove still called;

The flowers leaned on themselves, the flowers in hollows;
And love, love sang toward.

5

To have the whole air!
The light, the full sun
Coming down on the flowerheads,
The tendrils turning slowly,
A slow snail-lifting, liquescent;
To be by the rose
Rising slowly out of its bed,
Still as a child in its first loneliness;
To see cyclamen veins become clearer in early sunlight,
And mist lifting out of the brown cattails;
To stare into the after-light, the glitter left on the lake's surface,
When the sun has fallen behind a wooded island;
To follow the drops sliding from a lifted oar,
Held up, while the rower breathes, and the small boat drifts quietly
    shoreward;
To know that light falls and fills, often without our knowing,
As an opaque vase fills to the brim from a quick pouring,
Fills and trembles at the edge yet does not flow over,
Still holding and feeding the stem of the contained flower.

PRAISE TO THE END!

1

It's dark in this wood, soft mocker.
For whom have I swelled like a seed?
What a bone-ache I have.
Father of tensions, I'm down to my skin at last.

It's a great day for the mice.
Prickle-me, tickle-me, close stems.
Bumpkin, he can dance alone.
Ooh, ooh, I'm a duke of eels.

> Arch my back, pretty-bones, I'm dead at both ends.
> Softly softly, you'll wake the clams.
> I'll feed the ghost alone.
> Father, forgive my hands.

The rings have gone from the pond.
The river's alone with its water.
All risings
Fall.

2

Where are you now, my bonny beating gristle,
My blue original dandy, numb with sugar?
Once I fished from the banks, leaf-light and happy:
On the rocks south of quiet, in the close regions of kissing,
I romped, lithe as a child, down the summery streets of my veins,
Strict as a seed, nippy and twiggy.
Now the water's low. The weeds exceed me.
It's necessary, among the flies and bananas, to keep a constant vigil,

For the attacks of false humility take sudden turns for the worse.
Lacking the candor of dogs, I kiss the departing air;
I'm untrue to my own excesses.

Rock me to sleep, the weather's wrong.
Speak to me, frosty beard.
Sing to me, sweet.

Mips and ma the mooly moo,
The likes of him is biting who,
A cow's a care and who's a coo?—
What footie does is final.

My dearest dear my fairest fair,
Your father tossed a cat in air,
Though neither you nor I was there,—
What footie does is final.

Be large as an owl, be slick as a frog,
Be good as a goose, be big as a dog,
Be sleek as a heifer, be long as a hog,—
What footie will do will be final.

I conclude! I conclude!
My dearest dust, I can't stay here.
I'm undone by the flip-flap of odious pillows.
An exact fall of waters has rendered me impotent.
I've been asleep in a bower of dead skin.
It's a piece of a prince I ate.
This salt can't warm a stone.
These lazy ashes.

3

The stones were sharp,
The wind came at my back;
Walked along the highway,
Mincing like a cat.

The sun came out;
The lake turned green;
Romped upon the goldy grass,
Aged thirteen.

The sky cracked open
The world I knew;
Lay like the cats do
Sniffing the dew.

    I dreamt I was all bones;
    The dead slept in my sleeve;
    Sweet Jesus tossed me back:
    I wore the sun with ease.

    The several sounds were low;
    The river ebbed and flowed:
    Desire was winter-calm,
    A moon away.

Such owly pleasures! Fish come first, sweet bird.
Skin's the least of me. Kiss this.
Is the eternal near, fondling?
I hear the sound of hands.

Can the bones breathe? This grave has an ear.
It's still enough for the knock of a worm.

I feel more than a fish.
Ghost, come closer.

4

Arch of air, my heart's original knock,
I'm awake all over:
I've crawled from the mire, alert as a saint or a dog;
I know the back-stream's joy, and the stone's eternal pulseless longing.
Felicity I cannot hoard.
My friend, the rat in the wall, brings me the clearest messages;
I bask in the bower of change;
The plants wave me in, and the summer apples;
My palm-sweat flashes gold;
Many astounds before, I lost my identity to a pebble;
The minnows love me, and the humped and spitting creatures.

I believe! I believe!—
In the sparrow, happy on gravel;
In the winter-wasp, pulsing its wings in the sunlight;
I have been somewhere else; I remember the sea-faced uncles.
I hear, clearly, the heart of another singing,
Lighter than bells,
Softer than water.

Wherefore, O birds and small fish, surround me.
Lave me, ultimate waters.
The dark showed me a face.
My ghosts are all gay.
The light becomes me.

UNFOLD! UNFOLD!

1

By snails, by leaps of frog, I came here, spirit.
Tell me, body without skin, does a fish sweat?
I can't crawl back through those veins,
I ache for another choice.
The cliffs! The cliffs! They fling me back.
Eternity howls in the last crags,
The field is no longer simple:
It's a soul's crossing time.
The dead speak noise.

2

It's time you stood up and asked
                     —Or sat down and did.
A tongue without song
                     —Can still whistle in a jug.
You're blistered all over
                     —Who cares? The old owl?
When you find the wind
                     —Look for the white fire.

3

What a whelm of proverbs, Mr. Pinch!
Are the entrails clear, immaculate cabbage?
The last time I nearly whispered myself away.
I was far back, farther than anybody else.
On the jackpine plains I hunted the bird nobody knows;
Fishing, I caught myself behind the ears.
Alone, in a sleep-daze, I stared at billboards;

I was privy to oily fungus and the algae of standing waters;
Honored, on my return, by the ancient fellowship of rotten stems.
I was pure as a worm on a leaf; I cherished the mold's children.
Beetles sweetened my breath.
I slept like an insect.

I met a collector of string, a shepherd of slow forms.
My mission became the salvation of minnows.
I stretched like a board, almost a tree.
Even thread had a speech.

Later, I did and I danced in the simple wood.
A mouse taught me how, I was a happy asker.
Quite-by-chance brought me many cookies.
I jumped in butter.
Hair had kisses.

4

Easy the life of the mouth. What a lust for ripeness!
All openings praise us, even oily holes.
The bulb unravels. Who's floating? Not me.
The eye perishes in the small vision.
What else has the vine loosened?
I hear a dead tongue halloo.

5

Sing, sing, you symbols! All simple creatures,
All small shapes, willow-shy,
In the obscure haze, sing!

A light song comes from the leaves.
A slow sigh says yes. And light sighs;

A low voice, summer-sad.
Is it you, cold father? Father,
For whom the minnows sang?

A house for wisdom; a field for revelation.
Speak to the stones, and the stars answer.
At first the visible obscures:
Go where light is.

This fat can't laugh.
Only my salt has a chance.
I'll seek my own meekness.
What grace I have is enough.
The lost have their own pace.
The stalks ask something else.
What the grave says,
The nest denies.

In their harsh thickets
The dead thrash.
They help.

I CRY, LOVE! LOVE!

1

Went weeping, little bones. But where?
Wasps come when I ask for pigeons.
The sister sands, they slipper soft away.
What else can befall?

Delight me otherly, white spirit,—
Some errand, obscure as the wind's circuit,
A secret to jerk from the lips of a fish.
Is circularity such a shame?
A cat goes wider.

What's a thick? Two-by-two's a shape.
This toad could waltz on a drum;
I hear a most lovely huzza:
I'm king of the boops!

2

Reason? That dreary shed, that hutch for grubby schoolboys!
The hedgewren's song says something else.
I care for a cat's cry and the hugs, live as water.
I've traced these words in sand with a vestigial tail;
Now the gills are beginning to cry.
Such a sweet noise: I can't sleep for it.
Bless me and the maze I'm in!
Hello, thingy spirit.

Mouse, mouse, come out of the ferns,
And small mouths, stay your aimless cheeping:
A lapful of apples sleeps in this grass.

That anguish of concreteness!—
The sun playing on loam,
And the first dust of spring listing over backlots,—
I proclaim once more a condition of joy.
Walk into the wind, willie!

In a sodden place, all raps and knocks approve.
A dry cry comes from my own desert;
The bones are lonely.
Beginnings start without shade,
Thinner than minnows.
The live grass whirls with the sun,
Feet run over the simple stones,
There's time enough.
Behold, in the lout's eye,
Love.

3

I hear the owls, the soft callers, coming down from the hemlocks.
The bats weave in and out of the willows,
Wing-crooked and sure,
Downward and upward,
Dipping and veering close to the motionless water.

A fish jumps, shaking out flakes of moonlight.
A single wave starts lightly and easily shoreward,
Wrinkling between reeds in shallower water,
Lifting a few twigs and floating leaves,
Then washing up over small stones.

The shine on the face of the lake
Tilts, backward and forward.

The water recedes slowly,
Gently rocking.

Who untied the tree? I remember now.
We met in a nest. Before I lived.
The dark hair sighed.
We never enter
Alone.

O, THOU OPENING, O

I'll make it; but it may take me.
The rat's my phase.
My left side's tender.
Read me the stream.

Dazzle me, dizzy aphorist.
Fling me a precept.
I'm a draft sleeping by a stick;
I'm lost in what I have.

  The Depth calls to the Height
   —Neither knows it.
  Those close to the Ground
   —Only stay out of the Wind.

Thrum-thrum, who can be equal to ease?
I've seen my father's face before
Deep in the belly of a thing to be.
The Devil isn't dead; he's just away.

Where's Ann? Where's Lou? Where's Jock-with-the-Wind?
Forgive me a minute, nymph.
I'll change the image, and my shoes.
A true mole wanders like a worm.

2

And now are we to have that pelludious Jesus-shimmer over all
things, the animal's candid gaze, a shade less than feathers, light's
broken speech revived, a ghostly going of tame bears, a bright moon

on gleaming skin, a thing you cannot say to whisper and equal a Wound?

I'm tired of all that, Bag-Foot. I can hear small angels anytime. Who cares about the dance of dead underwear, or the sad waltz of paper bags? Who ever said God sang in your fat shape? You're not the only keeper of hay. That's a spratling's prattle. And don't be thinking you're simplicity's sweet thing, either. A leaf could drag you.

Where's the great rage of a rocking heart, the high rare true dangerous indignation? Let me persuade more slowly:

> The dark has its own light.
> A son has many fathers.
> Stand by a slow stream:
> Hear the sigh of what is.
> Be a pleased rock
> On a plain day.
> Waking's
> Kissing.
> Yes.

3

> You mean?—
> I can leap, true to the field,
> In the lily's sovereign right?
> Be a body lighted with love,
> Sad, in a singing-time?
> Or happy, correct as a hat?
>
> Oh, what a webby wonder I am!
> Swaying, would you believe,
> Like a sapling tree,
> Enough to please a cloud!

This frog's had another fall.
The old stalk still has a pulse;
I've crept from a cry.
The holy root wags the tail of a hill;
I'm true to soup, and happy to ask:
I sing the green, and things to come,
I'm king of another condition,
So alive I could die!
The ground's beating like flame!
You fat unnecessary hags,
You enemies of skin,—
A dolphin's at my door!
I'm twinkling like a twig!
The lark's my heart!
I'm wild with news!
My fancy's white!
I am my faces,
Love.

    Who reads in bed
        —Fornicates on the stove.
    An old dog
        —Should sleep on his paws.

See what the sweet harp says.
Should a song break a sleep?
The round home of a root,—
Is that the place to go?
I'm a tune dying
On harsh stone.
An Eye says,
Come.

I keep dreaming of bees.
This flesh has airy bones.
Going is knowing.
I see; I seek;
I'm near.
Be true,
Skin.

SHORTER POEMS
1951-1953

THE VISITANT

1

A cloud moved close. The bulk of the wind shifted.
A tree swayed over water.
A voice said:
Stay. Stay by the slip-ooze. Stay.

Dearest tree, I said, may I rest here?
A ripple made a soft reply.
I waited, alert as a dog.
The leech clinging to a stone waited;
And the crab, the quiet breather.

2

Slow, slow as a fish she came,
Slow as a fish coming forward,
Swaying in a long wave;
Her skirts not touching a leaf,
Her white arms reaching towards me.

She came without sound,
Without brushing the wet stones,
In the soft dark of early evening,
She came,
The wind in her hair,
The moon beginning.

3

I woke in the first of morning.
Staring at a tree, I felt the pulse of a stone.

Where's she now, I kept saying.
Where's she now, the mountain's downy girl?

But the bright day had no answer.
A wind stirred in a web of appleworms;
The tree, the close willow, swayed.

A LIGHT BREATHER

The spirit moves,
Yet stays:
Stirs as a blossom stirs,
Still wet from its bud-sheath,
Slowly unfolding,
Turning in the light with its tendrils;
Plays as a minnow plays,
Tethered to a limp weed, swinging,
Tail around, nosing in and out of the current,
Its shadows loose, a watery finger;
Moves, like the snail,
Still inward,
Taking and embracing its surroundings,
Never wishing itself away,
Unafraid of what it is,
A music in a hood,
A small thing,
Singing.

ELEGY FOR JANE
My Student, Thrown by a Horse

I remember the neckcurls, limp and damp as tendrils;
And her quick look, a sidelong pickerel smile;
And how, once startled into talk, the light syllables leaped for her,
And she balanced in the delight of her thought,
A wren, happy, tail into the wind,
Her song trembling the twigs and small branches.
The shade sang with her;
The leaves, their whispers turned to kissing;
And the mold sang in the bleached valleys under the rose.

Oh, when she was sad, she cast herself down into such a pure depth,
Even a father could not find her:
Scraping her cheek against straw;
Stirring the clearest water.

My sparrow, you are not here,
Waiting like a fern, making a spiny shadow.
The sides of wet stones cannot console me,
Nor the moss, wound with the last light.

If only I could nudge you from this sleep,
My maimed darling, my skittery pigeon.
Over this damp grave I speak the words of my love:
I, with no rights in this matter,
Neither father nor lover.

To seize, to seize,—
I know that dream.
Now my ardors sleep in a sleeve.
My eyes have forgotten.
Like the half-dead, I hug my last secrets.
O for some minstrel of what's to be,
A bird singing into the beyond,
The marrow of God, talking,
Full merry, a gleam
Gracious and bland,
On a bright stone.
Somewhere, among the ferns and birds,
The great swamps flash.
I would hold high converse
Where the winds gather,
And leap over my eye,
An old woman
Jumping in her shoes.
If only I could remember
The white grass bending away,
The doors swinging open,
The smells, the moment of hay,—
When I went to sea in a sigh,
In a boat of beautiful things.
The good day has gone:
The fair house, the high
Elm swinging around
With its deep shade, and birds.
I have listened close
For the thin sound in the windy chimney,
The fall of the last ash

From the dying ember.
I've become a sentry of small seeds,
Poking alone in my garden.
The stone walks, where are they?
Gone to bolster a road.
The shrunken soil
Has scampered away in a dry wind.
Once I was sweet with the light of myself,
A self-delighting creature,
Leaning over a rock,
My hair between me and the sun,
The waves rippling near me.
My feet remembered the earth,
The loam heaved me
That way and this.
My looks had a voice;
I was careless in growing.

If I were a young man,
I could roll in the dust of a fine rage.

The shadows are empty, the sliding externals.
The wind wanders around the house
On its way to the back pasture.
The cindery snow ticks over stubble.
My dust longs for the invisible.
I'm reminded to stay alive
By the dry rasp of the recurring inane,
The fine soot sifting through my south windows.
It is hard to care about corners,
And the sound of paper tearing.
I fall, more and more,
Into my own silences.
In the cold air,

The spirit
Hardens.

FOUR FOR SIR JOHN DAVIES

1 *The Dance*

Is that dance slowing in the mind of man
That made him think the universe could hum?
The great wheel turns its axle when it can;
I need a place to sing, and dancing-room,
And I have made a promise to my ears
I'll sing and whistle romping with the bears.

For they are all my friends: I saw one slide
Down a steep hillside on a cake of ice,—
Or was that in a book? I think with pride:
A caged bear rarely does the same thing twice
In the same way: O watch his body sway!—
This animal remembering to be gay.

I tried to fling my shadow at the moon,
The while my blood leaped with a wordless song.
Though dancing needs a master, I had none
To teach my toes to listen to my tongue.
But what I learned there, dancing all alone,
Was not the joyless motion of a stone.

I take this cadence from a man named Yeats;
I take it, and I give it back again:
For other tunes and other wanton beats
Have tossed my heart and fiddled through my brain.
Yes, I was dancing-mad, and how
That came to be the bears and Yeats would know.

2 *The Partner*

Between such animal and human heat
I find myself perplexed. What is desire?—
The impulse to make someone else complete?
That woman would set sodden straw on fire.
Was I the servant of a sovereign wish,
Or ladle rattling in an empty dish?

We played a measure with commingled feet:
The lively dead had taught us to be fond.
Who can embrace the body of his fate?
Light altered light along the living ground.
She kissed me close, and then did something else.
My marrow beat as wildly as my pulse.

I'd say it to my horse: we live beyond
Our outer skin. Who's whistling up my sleeve?
I see a heron prancing in his pond;
I know a dance the elephants believe.
The living all assemble! What's the cue?—
Do what the clumsy partner wants to do!

Things loll and loiter. Who condones the lost?
This joy outleaps the dog. Who cares? Who cares?
I gave her kisses back, and woke a ghost.
O what lewd music crept into our ears!
The body and the soul know how to play
In that dark world where gods have lost their way.

3 *The Wraith*

Incomprehensible gaiety and dread
Attended what we did. Behind, before,

Lay all the lonely pastures of the dead;
The spirit and the flesh cried out for more.
We two, together, on a darkening day
Took arms against our own obscurity.

Did each become the other in that play?
She laughed me out, and then she laughed me in;
In the deep middle of ourselves we lay;
When glory failed, we danced upon a pin.
The valley rocked beneath the granite hill;
Our souls looked forth, and the great day stood still.

There was a body, and it cast a spell,—
God pity those but wanton to the knees,—
The flesh can make the spirit visible;
We woke to find the moonlight on our toes.
In the rich weather of a dappled wood
We played with dark and light as children should.

What shape leaped forward at the sensual cry?—
Sea-beast or bird flung toward the ravaged shore?
Did space shake off an angel with a sigh?
We rose to meet the moon, and saw no more.
It was and was not she, a shape alone,
Impaled on light, and whirling slowly down.

4 *The Vigil*

Dante attained the purgatorial hill,
Trembled at hidden virtue without flaw,
Shook with a mighty power beyond his will,—
Did Beatrice deny what Dante saw?

All lovers live by longing, and endure:
Summon a vision and declare it pure.

Though everything's astonishment at last,
Who leaps to heaven at a single bound?
The links were soft between us; still, we kissed;
We undid chaos to a curious sound:
The waves broke easy, cried to me in white;
Her look was morning in the dying light.

The visible obscures. But who knows when?
Things have their thought: they are the shards of me;
I thought that once, and thought comes round again;
Rapt, we leaned forth with what we could not see.
We danced to shining; mocked before the black
And shapeless night that made no answer back.

The world is for the living. Who are they?
We dared the dark to reach the white and warm.
She was the wind when wind was in my way;
Alive at noon, I perished in her form.
Who rise from flesh to spirit know the fall:
The word outleaps the world, and light is all.

THE WAKING

I wake to sleep, and take my waking slow.
I feel my fate in what I cannot fear.
I learn by going where I have to go.

We think by feeling. What is there to know?
I hear my being dance from ear to ear.
I wake to sleep, and take my waking slow.

Of those so close beside me, which are you?
God bless the Ground! I shall walk softly there,
And learn by going where I have to go.

Light takes the Tree; but who can tell us how?
The lowly worm climbs up a winding stair;
I wake to sleep, and take my waking slow.

Great Nature has another thing to do
To you and me; so take the lively air,
And, lovely, learn by going where to go.

This shaking keeps me steady. I should know.
What falls away is always. And is near.
I wake to sleep, and take my waking slow.
I learn by going where I have to go.

PART TWO

NEW
POEMS

LIGHTER PIECES AND POEMS FOR CHILDREN

an interlude

SONG FOR THE SQUEEZE-BOX

It wasn't Ernest; it wasn't Scott—
The boys I knew when I went to pot;
They didn't boast; they didn't snivel,
But stepped right up and swung at the Devil;
And after exchanging a punch or two,
They all sat down like me and you
—And began to drink up the money.

It wasn't the Colony; it wasn't the Stork;
It wasn't the joints in New York, New York;
But me and a girl friend learned a lot
In Ecorse, Toledo, and Wyandotte
—About getting rid of our money.

It was jump-in-the-hedge; it was wait-in-the-hall;
It was "Would you believe it—*fawther's* talll"
(It turned out she hadn't a father at all)
—But how she could burn up the money!

A place I surely did like to go
Was the underbelly of Cicero;
And East St. Louis and Monongahela
Had the red-hot spots where you feel a
—Lot like losing some money.

Oh, the Synco Septet played for us then,
And even the boys turned out to be men
As we sat there drinking that bathtub gin
—And loosened up with our money.

It was Samoots Matuna and Bugs Moran;
It was Fade me another and Stick out your can;

It was Place and Show and Also Ran
—For you never won with that money.

Oh, it wasn't a crime, it wasn't a sin,
And nobody slipped me a Mickey Finn,
For whenever I could, I dealt them all in
—On that chunk of Grandpa's money.

It was Dead Man's Corner, it was Kelly's Stable;
It was Stand on your feet as long as you're able,
But many a man rolled under the table
—When he tried to drink up the money.

To some it may seem a sad thing to relate,
The dough I spent on Chippewa Kate,
For she finally left town on the Bay City freight
—When she thought I'd run out of money.

The doctors, the lawyers, the cops are all paid—
So I've got to get me a rich ugly old maid
Who isn't unwilling, who isn't afraid
—To help me eat up her money.

REPLY TO A LADY EDITOR

If the Poem (beginning "I knew a woman, lovely in her bones") in *The London Times Literary Supplement* has not appeared here, we offer you $75 for it. Could you wire us collect your answer?

Sincerely yours,
Alice S. Morris
Literary Editor, *Harper's Bazaar*

Sweet Alice S. Morris, I *am* pleased, of course,
You take the *Times Supplement*, and read its verse,
And know that True Love is more than a Life-Force
—And so like my poem called *Poem*.

Dan Cupid, I tell you's a braw laddie-buck;
A visit from him is a piece of pure luck,
And should he arrive, why just lean yourself back
—And recite him my poem called *Poem*.

O print it, my dear, do publish it, yes,
That ladies their true natures never suppress,
When they come, dazedly, to the pretty pass
—Of acting my poem called *Poem*.

My darling, my dearest, most-honest-alive,
Just send me along that sweet seventy-five;
I'll continue to think on the nature of love,
—As I dance to my poem called *Poem*.

DINKY

O what's the weather in a Beard?
It's windy there, and rather weird,
And when you think the sky has cleared
    —Why, there is Dirty Dinky.

Suppose you walk out in a Storm,
With nothing on to keep you warm,
And then step barefoot on a Worm
    —Of course, it's Dirty Dinky.

As I was crossing a hot hot Plain,
I saw a sight that caused me pain,
You asked me before, I'll tell you again:
    —It *looked* like Dirty Dinky.

Last night you lay a-sleeping? No!
The room was thirty-five below;
The sheets and blankets turned to snow.
    —He'd got in: Dirty Dinky.

You'd better watch the things you do,
You'd better watch the things you do.
You're part of him; he's part of you
    —*You* may be Dirty Dinky.

THE COW

There Once was a Cow with a Double Udder.
When I think of it now, I just have to Shudder!
She was too much for One, you can bet your Life:
She had to be Milked by a Man and his Wife.

THE SERPENT

There was a Serpent who had to sing.
There was. There was.
He simply gave up Serpenting.
Because. Because.

He didn't like his Kind of Life;
He couldn't find a proper Wife;
He was a Serpent with a soul;
He got no Pleasure down his Hole.
And so, of course, he had to Sing,
And Sing he did, like Anything!
The Birds, they were, they were Astounded;
And various Measures Propounded
To stop the Serpent's Awful Racket:
They bought a Drum. He wouldn't Whack it.
They sent,—you always send,—to Cuba
And got a Most Commodious Tuba;
They got a Horn, they got a Flute,
But Nothing would suit.
He said, "Look, Birds, all this is futile:
I do *not* like to Bang or Tootle."
And then he cut loose with a Horrible Note
That practically split the Top of his Throat.
"You see," he said, with a Serpent's Leer,
"I'm Serious about my Singing Career!"
And the Woods Resounded with many a Shriek
As the Birds flew off to the End of Next Week.

THE SLOTH

In moving-slow he has no Peer.
You ask him something in his Ear,
He thinks about it for a Year;

And, then, before he says a Word
There, upside down (unlike a Bird),
He will assume that you have Heard—

A most Ex-as-per-at-ing Lug.
But should you call his manner Smug,
He'll sigh and give his Branch a Hug;

Then off again to Sleep he goes,
Still swaying gently by his Toes,
And you just *know* he knows he knows.

THE LADY AND THE BEAR

A Lady came to a Bear by a Stream.
"O why are you fishing that way?
Tell me, dear Bear there by the Stream,
Why are you fishing that way?"

"I am what is known as a Biddly Bear,—
That's why I'm fishing this way.
We Biddly's are Pee-culiar Bears.
And so,—I'm fishing this way.

"And besides, it seems there's a Law:
A most, most exactious Law
Says a Bear
Doesn't dare
Doesn't dare
Doesn't DARE
Use a Hook or a Line,
Or an old piece of Twine,
Not even the end of his Claw, Claw, Claw,
Not even the end of his Claw.
Yes, a Bear has to fish with his Paw, Paw, Paw.
A Bear has to fish with his Paw."

"O it's Wonderful how with a flick of your Wrist,
You can fish out a fish, out a fish, out a fish,
If I were a fish I just couldn't resist
You, when you are fishing that way, that way,
When you are fishing that way."

And at that the Lady slipped from the Bank
And fell in the Stream still clutching a Plank,

But the Bear just sat there until she Sank;
As he went on fishing his way, his way,
As he went on fishing his way.

LOVE POEMS

THE DREAM

1

I met her as a blossom on a stem
Before she ever breathed, and in that dream
The mind remembers from a deeper sleep:
Eye learned from eye, cold lip from sensual lip.
My dream divided on a point of fire;
Light hardened on the water where we were;
A bird sang low; the moonlight sifted in;
The water rippled, and she rippled on.

2

She came toward me in the flowing air,
A shape of change, encircled by its fire.
I watched her there, between me and the moon;
The bushes and the stones danced on and on;
I touched her shadow when the light delayed;
I turned my face away, and yet she stayed.
A bird sang from the center of a tree;
She loved the wind because the wind loved me.

3

Love is not love until love's vulnerable.
She slowed to sigh, in that long interval.
A small bird flew in circles where we stood;
The deer came down, out of the dappled wood.
All who remember, doubt. Who calls that strange?
I tossed a stone, and listened to its plunge.
She knew the grammar of least motion, she
Lent me one virtue, and I live thereby.

4

She held her body steady in the wind;
Our shadows met, and slowly swung around;
She turned the field into a glittering sea;
I played in flame and water like a boy
And I swayed out beyond the white seafoam;
Like a wet log, I sang within a flame.
In that last while, eternity's confine,
I came to love, I came into my own.

1

I stand with standing stones.
The stones stay where they are.
The twiny winders wind;
The little fishes move.
A ripple wakes the pond.

2

This joy's my fall. I am!—
A man rich as a cat,
A cat in the fork of a tree,
When she shakes out her hair.
I think of that, and laugh.

3

All innocence and wit,
She keeps my wishes warm;
When, easy as a beast,
She steps along the street,
I start to leave myself.

4

The truly beautiful,
Their bodies cannot lie:
The blossom stings the bee.
The ground needs the abyss,
Say the stones, say the fish.

5

A field recedes in sleep.
Where are the dead? Before me
Floats a single star.
A tree glides with the moon.
The field is mine! Is mine!

6

In a lurking-place I lurk,
One with the sullen dark.
What's hell but a cold heart?
But who, faced with her face,
Would not rejoice?

1

Love, love, a lily's my care,
She's sweeter than a tree.
Loving, I use the air
Most lovingly: I breathe;
Mad in the wind I wear
Myself as I should be,
All's even with the odd,
My brother the vine is glad.

Are flower and seed the same?
What do the great dead say?
Sweet Phoebe, she's my theme:
She sways whenever I sway.
"O love me while I am,
You green thing in my way!"
I cried, and the birds came down
And made my song their own.

Motion can keep me still:
She kissed me out of thought
As a lovely substance will;
She wandered; I did not:
I stayed, and light fell
Across her pulsing throat;
I stared, and a garden stone
Slowly became the moon.

The shallow stream runs slack;
The wind creaks slowly by;
Out of a nestling's beak

Comes a tremulous cry
I cannot answer back;
A shape from deep in the eye—
That woman I saw in a stone—
Keeps pace when I walk alone.

2

The sun declares the earth;
The stones leap in the stream;
On a wide plain, beyond
The far stretch of a dream,
A field breaks like the sea;
The wind's white with her name,
And I walk with the wind.

The dove's my will today.
She sways, half in the sun:
Rose, easy on a stem,
One with the sighing vine,
One to be merry with,
And pleased to meet the moon.
She likes wherever I am.

Passion's enough to give
Shape to a random joy:
I cry delight: I know
The root, the core of a cry.
Swan-heart, arbutus-calm,
She moves when time is shy:
Love has a thing to do.

A fair thing grows more fair;
The green, the springing green

Makes an intenser day
Under the rising moon;
I smile, no mineral man; — *not dead*
I bear, but not alone,
The burden of this joy.

3

Under a southern wind,
The birds and fishes move
North, in a single stream;
The sharp stars swing around;
I get a step beyond
The wind, and there I am,
I'm odd and full of love.

Wisdom, where is it found?— } *not from God*
Those who embrace, believe.
Whatever was, still is, — *immortality*
Says a song tied to a tree.
Below, on the ferny ground,
In rivery air, at ease,
I walk with my true love.

What time's my heart? I care.
I cherish what I have
Had of the temporal:
I am no longer young
But the winds and waters are;
What falls away will fall;
All things bring me to love.

4

The breath of a long root,
The shy perimeter
Of the unfolding rose,
The green, the altered leaf,
The oyster's weeping foot,
And the incipient star—
Are part of what she is.
She wakes the ends of life.

Being myself, I sing
The soul's immediate joy.
Light, light, where's my repose?
A wind wreathes round a tree.
A thing is done: a thing
Body and spirit know
When I do what she does:
Creaturely creature, she!—

I kiss her moving mouth,
Her swart hilarious skin;
She breaks my breath in half;
She frolicks like a beast;
And I dance round and round,
A fond and foolish man,
And see and suffer myself
In another being, at last.

I KNEW A WOMAN

I knew a woman, lovely in her bones,
When small birds sighed, she would sigh back at them;
Ah, when she moved, she moved more ways than one:
The shapes a bright container can contain!
Of her choice virtues only gods should speak,
Or English poets who grew up on Greek
(I'd have them sing in chorus, cheek to cheek).

How well her wishes went! She stroked my chin,
She taught me Turn, and Counter-turn, and Stand;
She taught me Touch, that undulant white skin;
I nibbled meekly from her proffered hand;
She was the sickle; I, poor I, the rake,
Coming behind her for her pretty sake
(But what prodigious mowing we did make).

Love likes a gander, and adores a goose:
Her full lips pursed, the errant note to seize;
She played it quick, she played it light and loose;
My eyes, they dazzled at her flowing knees;
Her several parts could keep a pure repose,
Or one hip quiver with a mobile nose
(She moved in circles, and those circles moved).

Let seed be grass, and grass turn into hay:
I'm martyr to a motion not my own;
What's freedom for? To know eternity. see p. 144
I swear she cast a shadow white as stone.
But who would count eternity in days?
These old bones live to learn her wanton ways:
(I measure time by how a body sways).

THE VOICE

One feather is a bird,
I claim; one tree, a wood;
In her low voice I heard
More than a mortal should;
And so I stood apart,
Hidden in my own heart.

And yet I roamed out where
Those notes went, like the bird,
Whose thin song hung in air,
Diminished, yet still heard:
I lived with open sound,
Aloft, and on the ground.

That ghost was my own choice,
The shy cerulean bird;
It sang with her true voice,
And it was I who heard
A slight voice reply;
I heard; and only I.

Desire exults the ear:
Bird, girl, and ghostly tree,
The earth, the solid air—
Their slow song sang in me;
The long noon pulsed away,
Like any summer day.

SHE

I think the dead are tender. Shall we kiss?—
My lady laughs, delighting in what is.
If she but sighs, a bird puts out its tongue.
She makes space lonely with a lovely song.
She lilts a low soft language, and I hear
Down long sea-chambers of the inner ear.

We sing together; we sing mouth to mouth.
The garden is a river flowing south.
She cries out loud the soul's own secret joy;
She dances, and the ground bears her away.
She knows the speech of light, and makes it plain
A lively thing can come to life again.

I feel her presence in the common day,
In that slow dark that widens every eye.
She moves as water moves, and comes to me,
Stayed by what was, and pulled by what would be.

THE OTHER

What is she, while I live?—
Who plagues me with her Shape,
Lifting a nether Lip
Lightly: so buds unleave;
But if I move too close,
Who busks me on the Nose?

Is she what I become?
Is this my final Face?
I find her every place;
She happens, time on time—
My Nose feels for my Toe;
Nature's too much to know.

Who can surprise a thing
Or come to love alone?
A lazy natural man,
I loll, I loll, all Tongue.
She moves, and I adore:
Motion can do no more.

A child stares past a fire
With the same absent gaze:
I know her careless ways!—
Desire hides from desire.
Aging, I sometimes weep,
Yet still laugh in my sleep.

THE SENTENTIOUS MAN

1

Spirit and nature beat in one breast-bone—
I saw a virgin writhing in the dirt—
The serpent's heart sustains the loveless stone:
My indirection found direction out.

Pride in fine lineaments precedes a fall;
True lechers love the flesh, and that is all.

2

We did not fly the flesh. Who does, when young?
A fire leaps on itself: I know that flame.
Some rages save us. Did I rage too long?
The spirit knows the flesh it must consume.

The dream's an instant that calls up her face.
She changed me ice to fire, and fire to ice.

3

Small waves repeat the mind's slow sensual play.
I stay alive, both in and out of time,
By listening to the spirit's smallest cry;
In the long night, I rest within her name—

As if a lion knelt to kiss a rose,
Astonished into passionate repose.

4

Though all's in motion, who is passing by?
The after-image never stays the same.
There was a thicket where I went to die,
And there I thrashed, my thighs and face aflame.

But my least motion changed into a song,
And all dimensions quivered to one thing.

5

An exultation takes us outside life:
I can delight in my own hardihood;
I taste my sister when I kiss my wife;
I drink good liquor when my luck is good.

A drunkard drinks, and belches in his drink;
Such ardor tames eternity, I think.

6

Is pain a promise? I was schooled in pain,
And found out all I could of all desire;
I weep for what I'm like when I'm alone
In the deep center of the voice and fire.

I know the motion of the deepest stone.
Each one's himself, yet each one's everyone.

7

I'm tired of brooding on my neighbor's soul;
My friends become more Christian, year by year.

Small waters run toward a miry hole—
That's not a thing I'm saying with a sneer—

For water moves until it's purified,
And the weak bridegroom strengthens in his bride.

THE PURE FURY

1

Stupor of knowledge lacking inwardness—
What book, O learned man, will set me right?
Once I read nothing through a fearful night,
For every meaning had grown meaningless.
Morning, I saw the world with second sight,
As if all things had died, and rose again.
I touched the stones, and they had my own skin.

2

The pure admire the pure, and live alone;
I love a woman with an empty face.
Parmenides put Nothingness in place;
She tries to think, and it flies loose again.
How slow the changes of a golden mean:
Great Boehme rooted all in Yes and No;
At times my darling squeaks in pure Plato.

3

How terrible the need for solitude:
That appetite for life so ravenous
A man's a beast prowling in his own house,
A beast with fangs, and out for his own blood
Until he finds the thing he almost was
When the pure fury first raged in his head
And trees came closer with a denser shade.

4

Dream of a woman, and a dream of death:
The light air takes my being's breath away;
I look on white, and it turns into gray—
When will that creature give me back my breath?
I live near the abyss. I hope to stay
Until my eyes look at a brighter sun   *until he*
As the thick shade of the long night comes on.   *believes in God*

THE RENEWAL

1

What glories would we? Motions of the soul?
The centaur and the sybil romp and sing
Within the reach of my imagining:
Such affirmations are perpetual.
I teach my sighs to lengthen into songs,
Yet, like a tree, endure the shift of things.

2

The night wind rises. Does my father live?
Dark hangs upon the waters of the soul;
My flesh is breathing slower than a wall.
Love alters all. Unblood my instinct, love.
These waters drowse me into sleep so kind
I walk as if my face would kiss the wind.

3

Sudden renewal of the self—from where?
A raw ghost drinks the fluid in my spine;
I know I love, yet know not where I am;
I paw the dark, the shifting midnight air.
Will the self, lost, be found again? In form?
I walk the night to keep my five wits warm.

4

Dry bones! Dry bones! I find my loving heart,
Illumination brought to such a pitch
I see the rubblestones begin to stretch

As if reality had split apart
And the whole motion of the soul lay bare:
I find that love, and I am everywhere.

"There is no place to turn," she said,
    "You have me pinned so close;
My hair's all tangled on your head,
    My back is just one bruise;
I feel we're breathing with the dead;
    O angel, let me loose!"

And she was right, for there beside
    The gin and cigarettes,
A woman stood, pure as a bride,
    Affrighted from her wits,
And breathing hard, as that man rode
    Between those lovely tits.

"My shoulder's bitten from your teeth;
    What's that peculiar smell?
No matter which one is beneath,
    Each is an animal,"—
The ghostly figure sucked its breath,
    And shuddered toward the wall;
Wrapped in the tattered robe of death,
    It tiptoed down the hall.

"The bed itself begins to quake,
    I hate this sensual pen;
My neck, if not my heart, will break
    If we do this again,"—
Then each fell back, limp as a sack,
    Into the world of men.

LOVE'S PROGRESS

1

The possibles we dare!
O rare propinquity!—
I have considered and found
A mouth I cannot leave.
The great gods arch my bones.

2

The long veins of the vine
Journey around a tree;
Light strides the rose;
A woman's naked in water,
And I know where she is.

3

True, she can think a bird
Until it broods in her eyes.
Love me, my violence,
Light of my spirit, light
Beyond the look of love.

4

It's midnight on the mouse,
The rabbit, and the wren;
A log sings in its flame.
Father, I'm far from home,
And I have gone nowhere.

5

The close dark hugs me hard,
And all the birds are stone.
I fear for my own joy;
I fear myself in the field,
For I would drown in fire.

THE SURLY ONE

1

When true love broke my heart in half,
I took the whiskey from the shelf,
And told my neighbors when to laugh.
I keep a dog, and bark myself.

2

Ghost cries out to ghost—
But who's afraid of that?
I fear those shadows most
That start from my own feet.

PLAINT

Day after somber day,
I think my neighbors strange;
In hell there is no change. → *broken heart*
Where's my eternity
Of inward blessedness?
I lack plain tenderness.

Where is the knowledge that
Could bring me to my God? *not in return*
Not on this dusty road
Or afternoon of light
Diminished by the haze
Of late November days.

I lived with deep roots once:
Have I forgotten their ways—
The gradual embrace
Of lichen around stones?
Death is a deeper sleep,
And I delight in sleep.

THE SWAN

1

I study out a dark similitude:
Her image fades, yet does not disappear—
Must I stay tangled in that lively hair?
Is there no way out of that coursing blood?
A dry soul's wisest. O, I am not dry!
My darling does what I could never do:
She sighs me white, a Socrates of snow.

We think too long in terms of what to be;
I live, alive and certain as a bull;
A casual man, I keep my casual word,
Yet whistle back at every whistling bird.
A man alive, from all light I must fall.
I am my father's son, I am John Donne
Whenever I see her with nothing on.

2

The moon draws back its waters from the shore.
By the lake's edge, I see a silver swan,
And she is what I would. In this light air,
Lost opposites bend down—
Sing of that nothing of which all is made,
Or listen into silence, like a god.

MEMORY

1

In the slow world of dream,
We breathe in unison.
The outside dies within,
And she knows all I am.

2

She turns, as if to go,
Half-bird, half-animal.
The wind dies on the hill.
Love's all. Love's all I know.

3

A doe drinks by a stream,
A doe and its fawn.
When I follow after them,
The grass changes to stone.

VOICES AND CREATURES

"THE SHIMMER OF EVIL" *Louise Bogan*

The weather wept, and all the trees bent down;
Bent down their birds: the light waves took the waves;
Each single substance gliddered to the stare;
Each vision purely, purely was its own:
—There was no light; there was no light at all:

Far from the mirrors all the bushes rang
With their hard snow; leaned on the lonely eye;
Cold evil twinkled tighter than a string; a fire
Hung down: And I was only I.
—There was no light; there was no light at all:

Each cushion found itself a field of pins,
Prickling pure wishes with confusion's ire;
Hope's holy wrists: the little burning boys
Cried out their lives an instant and were free.
—There was no light; there was no light at all.

ELEGY

1

Should every creature be as I have been,
There would be reason for essential sin;
I have myself an inner weight of woe
That God himself can scarcely bear.

2

Each wills his death: I am convinced of that;
You were too lonely for another fate.
I have myself an inner weight of woe
That Christ, securely bound, could bear.

3

Thus I; and should these reasons fly apart,
I know myself, my seasons, and I KNOW.
I have myself one crumbling skin to show;
God could believe: I am here to fear.

4

What you survived I shall believe: the Heat,
Scars, Tempests, Floods, the Motion of Man's Fate;
I have myself, and bear its weight of woe
That God that God leans down His heart to hear.

THE BEAST

I came to a great door,
Its lintel overhung
With burr, bramble, and thorn;
And when it swung, I saw
A meadow, lush and green.

And there a great beast played,
A sportive, aimless one,
A shred of bone its horn,
And colloped round with fern.
It looked at me; it stared.

Swaying, I took its gaze;
Faltered; rose up again;
Rose but to lurch and fall,
Hard, on the gritty sill,
I lay; I languished there.

When I raised myself once more,
The great round eyes had gone.
The long lush grass lay still;
And I wept there, alone.

THE SONG

1

I met a ragged man;
He looked beyond me when
I tried to meet his eyes.
What have I done to you?
I cried, and backed away.
Dust in a corner stirred,
And the walls stretched wide.

2

I went running down a road,
In a country of bleak stone,
And shocks of ragged corn;
When I stayed for breath, I lay
With the saxifrage and fern
At the edge of a raw field.
I stared at a fissure of ground
Ringed round with crumbled clay:
The old house of a crab;
Stared, and began to sing.

3

I sang to whatever had been
Down in that watery hole:
I wooed with a low tune;
You could say I was mad.
And a wind woke in my hair,
And the sweat poured from my face,
When I heard, or thought I heard,

Another join my song
With the small voice of a child,
Close, and yet far away.

Mouth upon mouth, we sang,
My lips pressed upon stone.

THE EXORCISM

1

The gray sheep came. I ran,
My body half in flame.
(Father of flowers, who
Dares face the thing he is?)

As if pure being woke,
The dust rose and spoke;
A shape cried from a cloud,
Cried to my flesh out loud.

(And yet I was not there,
But down long corridors,
My own, my secret lips
Babbling in urinals.)

2

In a dark wood I saw—
I saw my several selves
Come running from the leaves,
Lewd, tiny, careless lives
That scuttled under stones,
Or broke, but would not go.
I turned upon my spine,
I turned and turned again,
A cold God-furious man
Writhing until the last
Forms of his secret life
Lay with the dross of death.

I was myself, alone.

I broke from that low place
Breathing a slower breath,
Cold, in my own dead salt.

The small birds swirl around;
The high cicadas chirr;
A towhee pecks the ground;
I look at the first star:
My heart held to its joy,
This whole September day.

The moon goes to the full;
The moon goes slowly down;
The wood becomes a wall.
Far things draw closer in.
A wind moves through the grass,
Then all is as it was.

What rustles in the fern?
I feel my flesh divide.
Things lost in sleep return
As if out of my side,
On feet that make no sound
Over the sodden ground.

The small shapes drowse: I live
To woo the fearful small;
What moves in grass I love—
The dead will not lie still,
And things throw light on things,
And all the stones have wings.

A WALK IN LATE SUMMER

1

A gull rides on the ripples of a dream,
White upon white, slow-settling on a stone;
Across my lawn the soft-backed creatures come;
In the weak light they wander, each alone.
Bring me the meek, for I would know their ways;
I am a connoisseur of midnight eyes.
The small! The small! I hear them singing clear
On the long banks, in the soft summer air.

2

What is there for the soul to understand?
The slack face of the dismal pure inane?
The wind dies down; my will dies with the wind,
God's in that stone, or I am not a man!
Body and soul transcend appearances
Before the caving-in of all that is;
I'm dying piecemeal, fervent in decay;
My moments linger—that's eternity.

3

A late rose ravages the casual eye,
A blaze of being on a central stem.
It lies upon us to undo the lie
Of living merely in the realm of time.
Existence moves toward a certain end—
A thing all earthly lovers understand.
That dove's elaborate way of coming near
Reminds me I am dying with the year.

4

A tree arises on a central plain—
It is no trick of change or chance of light.
A tree all out of shape from wind and rain,
A tree thinned by the wind obscures my sight.
The long day dies; I walk the woods alone;
Beyond the ridge two wood thrush sing as one.
Being delights in being, and in time.
The evening wraps me, steady as a flame.

SNAKE

I saw a young snake glide
Out of the mottled shade
And hang, limp on a stone:
A thin mouth, and a tongue
Stayed, in the still air.

It turned; it drew away;
Its shadow bent in half;
It quickened, and was gone.

I felt my slow blood warm.
I longed to be that thing,
The pure, sensuous form.

And I may be, some time.

SLUG

How I loved one like you when I was little!—
With his stripes of silver and his small house on his back,
Making a slow journey around the well-curb.
I longed to be like him, and was,
In my way, close cousin
To the dirt, my knees scrubbing
The gravel, my nose wetter than his.

When I slip, just slightly, in the dark,
I know it isn't a wet leaf,
But you, loose toe from the old life,
The cold slime come into being,
A fat, five-inch appendage
Creeping slowly over the wet grass,
Eating the heart out of my garden.

And you refuse to die decently!—
Flying upward through the knives of my lawnmower
Like pieces of smoked eel or raw oyster,
And I go faster in my rage to get done with it,
Until I'm scraping and scratching at you, on the doormat,
The small dead pieces sticking under an instep;
Or, poisoned, dragging a white skein of spittle over a path—
Beautiful, in its way, like quicksilver—
You shrink to something less,
A rain-drenched fly or spider.

I'm sure I've been a toad, one time or another.
With bats, weasels, worms—I rejoice in the kinship.
Even the caterpillar I can love, and the various vermin.
But as for you, most odious—
Would Blake call you holy?

THE SISKINS

The bank swallows veer and dip,
Diving down at my windows,
Then flying almost straight upward,
Like bats in daytime,
And their shadows, bigger,
Race over the thick grass;
And the finches pitch through the air, twittering;
And the small mad siskins flit by,
Flying upward in little skips and erratic leaps;
Or they sit sideways on limber dandelion stems,
Bending them down to the ground;
Or perch and peck at larger flower-crowns,
Springing, one to another,
The last-abandoned stalk always quivering
Back into straightness;
Or they fling themselves against tree trunks,
Scuttling down and around like young squirrels,
Birds furious as bees.

Now they move all together!—
These airy hippety-hop skippers,
Light as seed blowing off thistles!
And I seem to lean forward,
As my eyes follow after
Their sunlit leaping.

THE DYING MAN

In Memoriam: W. B. Yeats

THE DYING MAN

1 *His Words*

I heard a dying man
Say to his gathered kin,
"My soul's hung out to dry,
Like a fresh-salted skin;
I doubt I'll use it again.

"What's done is yet to come;
The flesh deserts the bone,
But a kiss widens the rose;
I know, as the dying know,
Eternity is Now.

"A man sees, as he dies,
Death's possibilities;
My heart sways with the world.
I am that final thing,
A man learning to sing."

2 *What Now?*

Caught in the dying light,
I thought myself reborn.
My hands turn into hooves.
I wear the leaden weight
Of what I did not do.

Places great with their dead,
The mire, the sodden wood,
Remind me to stay alive.

I am the clumsy man
The instant ages on.

I burned the flesh away,
In love, in lively May.
I turn my look upon
Another shape than hers
Now, as the casement blurs.

In the worst night of my will,
I dared to question all,
And would the same again.
What's beating at the gate?
Who's come can wait.

3   *The Wall*

A ghost comes out of the unconscious mind
To grope my sill: It moans to be reborn!
The figure at my back is not my friend;
The hand upon my shoulder turns to horn.
I found my father when I did my work,
Only to lose myself in this small dark.

Though it reject dry borders of the seen,
What sensual eye can keep an image pure,
Leaning across a sill to greet the dawn?
A slow growth is a hard thing to endure.
When figures out of obscure shadow rave,
All sensual love's but dancing on a grave.

The wall has entered: I must love the wall,
A madman staring at perpetual night,
A spirit raging at the visible.

I breathe alone until my dark is bright.
Dawn's where the white is. Who would know the dawn
When there's a dazzling dark behind the sun?

4   The Exulting

Once I delighted in a single tree;
The loose air sent me running like a child—
I love the world; I want more than the world,
Or after-image of the inner eye.
Flesh cries to flesh; and bone cries out to bone;
I die into this life, alone yet not alone.

Was it a god his suffering renewed?—
I saw my father shrinking in his skin;
He turned his face: there was another man,
Walking the edge, loquacious, unafraid.
He quivered like a bird in birdless air,
Yet dared to fix his vision anywhere.

Fish feed on fish, according to their need:
My enemies renew me, and my blood
Beats slower in my careless solitude.
I bare a wound, and dare myself to bleed.
I think a bird, and it begins to fly.
By dying daily, I have come to be.

All exultation is a dangerous thing.
I see you, love, I see you in a dream;
I hear a noise of bees, a trellis hum,
And that slow humming rises into song.
A breath is but a breath: I have the earth;
I shall undo all dying by my death.

5 *They Sing, They Sing*

All women loved dance in a dying light—
The moon's my mother: how I love the moon!
Out of her place she comes, a dolphin one,
Then settles back to shade and the long night.
A beast cries out as if its flesh were torn,
And that cry takes me back where I was born.

Who thought love but a motion in the mind?
Am I but nothing, leaning towards a thing?
I'll scare myself with sighing, or I'll sing;
Descend, O gentlest light, descend, descend.
O sweet field far ahead, I hear your birds,
They sing, they sing, but still in minor thirds.

I've the lark's word for it, who sings alone:
What's seen recedes; Forever's what we know!—
Eternity defined, and strewn with straw,
The fury of the slug beneath the stone.
The vision moves, and yet remains the same.
In heaven's praise, I dread the thing I am.

The edges of the summit still appal
When we brood on the dead or the beloved;
Nor can imagination do it all
In this last place of light: he dares to live
Who stops being a bird, yet beats his wings
Against the immense immeasurable emptiness of things.

MEDITATIONS OF
AN OLD WOMAN

FIRST MEDITATION

1

On love's worst ugly day,
The weeds hiss at the edge of the field,
The small winds make their chilly indictments.
Elsewhere, in houses, even pails can be sad;
While stones loosen on the obscure hillside,
And a tree tilts from its roots,
Toppling down an embankment.

The spirit moves, but not always upward,
While animals eat to the north,
And the shale slides an inch in the talus,
The bleak wind eats at the weak plateau,
And the sun brings joy to some.
But the rind, often, hates the life within.

How can I rest in the days of my slowness?
I've become a strange piece of flesh,
Nervous and cold, bird-furtive, whiskery,
With a cheek soft as a hound's ear.
What's left is light as a seed;
I need an old crone's knowing.

2

Often I think of myself as riding—
Alone, on a bus through western country.
I sit above the back wheels, where the jolts are hardest,
And we bounce and sway along toward the midnight,
The lights tilting up, skyward, as we come over a little rise,
Then down, as we roll like a boat from a wave-crest.

All journeys, I think, are the same:
The movement is forward, after a few wavers,
And for a while we are all alone,
Busy, obvious with ourselves,
The drunken soldier, the old lady with her peppermints;
And we ride, we ride, taking the curves
Somewhat closer, the trucks coming
Down from behind the last ranges,
Their black shapes breaking past;
And the air claps between us,
Blasting the frosted windows,
And I seem to go backward,
Backward in time:

    Two song sparrows, one within a greenhouse,
    Shuttling its throat while perched on a wind-vent,
    And another, outside, in the bright day,
    With a wind from the west and the trees all in motion.
    One sang, then the other,
    The songs tumbling over and under the glass,
    And the men beneath them wheeling in dirt to the cement
        benches,
    The laden wheelbarrows creaking and swaying,
    And the up-spring of the plank when a foot left the runway.

Journey within a journey:
The ticket mislaid or lost, the gate
Inaccessible, the boat always pulling out
From the rickety wooden dock,
The children waving;
Or two horses plunging in snow, their lines tangled,
A great wooden sleigh careening behind them,
Swerving up a steep embankment.
For a moment they stand above me,

Their black skins shuddering:
Then they lurch forward,
Lunging down a hillside.

3

As when silt drifts and sifts down through muddy pond-water,
Settling in small beads around weeds and sunken branches,
And one crab, tentative, hunches himself before moving along the
    bottom,
Grotesque, awkward, his extended eyes looking at nothing in particular,
Only a few bubbles loosening from the ill-matched tentacles,
The tail and smaller legs slipping and sliding slowly backward—
So the spirit tries for another life,
Another way and place in which to continue;
Or a salmon, tired, moving up a shallow stream,
Nudges into a back-eddy, a sandy inlet,
Bumping against sticks and bottom-stones, then swinging
Around, back into the tiny maincurrent, the rush of brownish-white
    water,
Still swimming forward—
So, I suppose, the spirit journeys.

4

I have gone into the waste lonely places
Behind the eye; the lost acres at the edge of smoky cities.
What's beyond never crumbles like an embankment,
Explodes like a rose, or thrusts wings over the Caribbean.
There are no pursuing forms, faces on walls:
Only the motes of dust in the immaculate hallways,
The darkness of falling hair, the warnings from lint and spiders,
The vines graying to a fine powder.
There is no riven tree, or lamb dropped by an eagle.

There are still times, morning and evening:
The cerulean, high in the elm,
Thin and insistent as a cicada,
And the far phoebe, singing,
The long plaintive notes floating down,
Drifting through leaves, oak and maple,
Or the whippoorwill, along the smoky ridges,
A single bird calling and calling;
A fume reminds me, drifting across wet gravel;
A cold wind comes over stones;
A flame, intense, visible,
Plays over the dry pods,
Runs fitfully along the stubble,
Moves over the field,
Without burning.
    In such times, lacking a god,
    I am still happy.

I'M HERE

1

Is it enough?—
The sun loosening the frost on December windows,
The glitter of wet in the first of morning?
The sound of voices, young voices, mixed with sleighbells,
Coming across snow in early evening?

Outside, the same sparrows bicker in the eaves.
I'm tired of tiny noises:
The April cheeping, the vireo's insistence,
The prattle of the young no longer pleases.
Behind the child's archness
Lurks the bad animal.

  —How needles and corners perplex me!
    Dare I shrink to a hag,
    The worst surprise a corner could have,
    A witch who sleeps with her horse?
    Some fates are worse.

2

I was queen of the vale—
For a short while,
Living all my heart's summer alone,
Ward of my spirit,
Running through high grasses,
My thighs brushing against flower-crowns;
Leaning, out of all breath,
Bracing my back against a sapling,
Making it quiver with my body;

At the stream's edge, trailing a vague finger;
Flesh-awkward, half-alive,
Fearful of high places, in love with horses;
In love with stuffs, silks,
Rubbing my nose in the wool of blankets;
Bemused; pleased to be;
Mindful of cries,
The meaningful whisper,
The wren, the catbird.

So much of adolescence is an ill-defined dying,
An intolerable waiting,
A longing for another place and time,
Another condition.

I stayed: a willow to the wind.
The bats twittered at noon.
The swallows flew in and out of the smokeless chimneys.
I sang to the edges of flame,
My skin whiter in the soft weather,
My voice softer.

3

I remember walking down a path,
Down wooden steps toward a weedy garden;
And my dress caught on a rose-brier.
When I bent to untangle myself,
The scent of the half-opened buds came up over me.
I thought I was going to smother.

In the slow coming-out of sleep,
On the sill of the eyes, something flutters,
A thing we feel at evening, and by doors,

Or when we stand at the edge of a thicket,
And the ground-chill comes closer to us,
From under the dry leaves,
A beachy wetness.

The body, delighting in thresholds,
Rocks in and out of itself.
A bird, small as a leaf,
Sings in the first
Sunlight.

And the time I was so sick—
The whole place shook whenever I got a chill—
I closed my eyes, and saw small figures dancing,
A congress of tree-shrews and rats,
Romping around a fire,
Jumping up and down on their hind feet,
Their forepaws joined together, like hands—
They seemed very happy.

In my grandmother's inner eye,
So she told me when I was little,
A bird always kept singing.
She was a serious woman.

4

My geranium is dying, for all I can do,
Still leaning toward the last place the sun was.
I've tried I don't know how many times to replant it.
But these roses: I can wear them by looking away.
The eyes rejoice in the act of seeing and the fresh after-image;
Without staring like a lout, or a moping adolescent;
Without commotion.

Look at the far trees at the end of the garden.
The flat branch of that hemlock holds the last of the sun,
Rocking it, like a sun-struck pond,
In a light wind.

I prefer the still joy:
The wasp drinking at the edge of my cup;
A snake lifting its head;
A snail's music.

5

What's weather to me? Even carp die in this river.
I need a pond with small eels. And a windy orchard.
I'm no midge of that and this. The dirt glitters like salt.
Birds are around. I've all the singing I would.
I'm not far from a stream.
It's not my first dying.
I can hold this valley,
Loose in my lap,
In my arms.

If the wind means me,
I'm here!
Here.

HER BECOMING

1

I have learned to sit quietly,
Watching the wind riffle the backs of small birds,
Chirping with fleas in the sand,
My shape a levity—Yes!—
A mad hen in a far corner of the dark,
Still taking delight in nakedness,
In the sun, busy at a young body,
In the rain, slackening on a summer field;
In the back of my mind, running with the rolling water,
My breast wild as the waves.

    I see a shape, lighted with love,
    Light as a petal falling upon stone.
    From the folds of my skin, I sing,
    The air still, the ground alive,
    The earth itself a tune.

How sweetly I abide. Am I a bird?
Soft, soft, the snow's not falling. What's a seed?
A face floats in the ferns. Do maimed gods walk?
A voice keeps rising in my early sleep,
A muffled voice, a low sweet watery noise.
Dare I embrace a ghost from my own breast?
A spirit plays before me like a child,
A child at play, a wind-excited bird.

    A ghost from the soul's house?
    I'm where I always was.
    The lily broods. Who knows
    The way out of a rose?

2

Is it the sea we wish? The sleep of the changeless?
In my left ear I hear the loud sound of a minor collapse.
Last night I dreamt of a jauntier principle of order;
Today I eat my usual diet of shadows.
Dare I speak, once more, in the monotony of great praise,
In the wild disordered language of the natural heart?
What else can I steal from sleep?

We start from the dark. Pain teaches us little.
I can't laugh from a crater of burning pitch,
Or live the dangerous life of an insect.
Is there a wisdom in objects? Few objects praise the Lord.
The bulks cannot hide us, or the bleak sheds of our desolation.
I know the cold fleshless kiss of contraries,
The nerveless constriction of surfaces—
Machines, machines, loveless, temporal;
Mutilated souls in cold morgues of obligation.

3

There are times when reality comes closer:
In a field, in the actual air,
I stepped carefully, like a new-shod horse,
A raw tumultuous girl
Making my way over wet stones.
And then I ran—
Ran ahead of myself,
Across a field, into a little wood.

And there I stayed until the day burned down.

My breath grew less. I listened like a beast.
Was it the stones I heard? I stared at the fixed stars.

The moon, a pure Islamic shape, looked down.
The light air slowed: It was not night or day.
All natural shapes became symbolical.
The only thing alive in heaven's eye,
I shed my clothes to slow my daemon down.
And then I ran again.

Where was I going? Where?
What was I running from?
To these I cried my life—
The loved fox, and the wren.

Speech passed between small birds;
Silence became a thing;
Echo itself consumed;
The scene shrank to a pin.

Did my will die? Did I?
I said farewell to sighs,
Once to the toad,
Once to the frog,
And once to my flowing thighs.

Who can believe the moon?
I have seen! I have seen!—
The line! The holy line!
A small place all in flame.

Out, out, you secret beasts,
You birds, you western birds.
One follows fire. One does.
My breath is more than yours.

What lover keeps his song?
I sigh before I sing.
I love because I am
A rapt thing with a name.

4

Ask all the mice who caper in the straw—
I am benign in my own company.
A shape without a shade, or almost none,
I hum in pure vibration, like a saw.
The grandeur of a crazy one alone!—
By swoops of bird, by leaps of fish, I live.
My shadow steadies in a shifting stream;
I live in air; the long light is my home;
I dare caress the stones, the field my friend;
A light wind rises: I become the wind.

FOURTH MEDITATION

1

I was always one for being alone,
Seeking in my own way, eternal purpose;
At the edge of the field waiting for the pure moment;
Standing, silent, on sandy beaches or walking along green embank-
    ments;
Knowing the sinuousness of small waters:
As a chip or shell, floating lazily with a slow current,
A drop of the night rain still in me,
A bit of water caught in a wrinkled crevice,
A pool riding and shining with the river,
Dipping up and down in the ripples,
Tilting back the sunlight.

Was it yesterday I stretched out the thin bones of my innocence?
O the songs we hide, singing only to ourselves!
Once I could touch my shadow, and be happy;
In the white kingdoms, I was light as a seed,
Drifting with the blossoms,
A pensive petal.

But a time comes when the vague life of the mouth no longer suffices;
The dead make more impossible demands from their silence;
The soul stands, lonely in its choice,
Waiting, itself a slow thing,
In the changing body.

The river moves, wrinkled by midges,
A light wind stirs in the pine needles.
The shape of a lark rises from a stone;
But there is no song.

2

What is it to be a woman?
To be contained, to be a vessel?
To prefer a window to a door?
A pool to a river?
To become lost in a love,
Yet remain only half aware of the intransient glory?
To be a mouth, a meal of meat?
To gaze at a face with the fixed eyes of a spaniel?

I think of the self-involved:
The ritualists of the mirror, the lonely drinkers,
The minions of benzedrine and paraldehyde,
And those who submerge themselves deliberately in trivia,
Women who become their possessions,
Shapes stiffening into metal,
Match-makers, arrangers of picnics—
What do their lives mean,
And the lives of their children?—
The young, brow-beaten early into a baleful silence,
Frozen by a father's lip, a mother's failure to answer.
Have they seen, ever, the sharp bones of the poor?
Or known, once, the soul's authentic hunger,
Those cat-like immaculate creatures
For whom the world works?

What do they need?
O more than a roaring boy,
For the sleek captains of intuition cannot reach them;
They feel neither the tearing iron
Nor the sound of another footstep—
How I wish them awake!
May the high flower of the hay climb into their hearts;
May they lean into light and live;

May they sleep in robes of green, among the ancient ferns;
May their eyes gleam with the first dawn;
May the sun gild them a worm;
May they be taken by the true burning;
May they flame into being!—

I see them as figures walking in a greeny garden,
Their gait formal and elaborate, their hair a glory,
The gentle and beautiful still-to-be-born;
The descendants of the playful tree-shrew that survived the archaic
    killers,
The fang and the claw, the club and the knout, the irrational edict,
The fury of the hate-driven zealot, the meanness of the human weasel;
Who turned a corner in time, when at last he grew a thumb;
A prince of small beginnings, enduring the slow stretches of change,
Who spoke first in the coarse short-hand of the subliminal depths,
Made from his terror and dismay a grave philosophical language;
A lion of flame, pressed to the point of love,
Yet moves gently among the birds.

3
Younglings, the small fish keep heading into the current.
What's become of care? This lake breathes like a rose.
Beguile me, change. What have I fallen from?
I drink my tears in a place where all light comes.
I'm in love with the dead! My whole forehead's a noise!
On a dark day I walk straight toward the rain.
Who else sweats light from a stone?
By singing we defend;
The husk lives on, ardent as a seed;
My back creaks with the dawn.

Is my body speaking? I breathe what I am:
The first and last of all things.
Near the graves of the great dead,
Even the stones speak.

WHAT CAN I TELL MY BONES?

1

Beginner,
Perpetual beginner,
The soul knows not what to believe,
In its small folds, stirring sluggishly,
In the least place of its life,
A pulse beyond nothingness,
A fearful ignorance.

　　Before the moon draws back,
　　Dare I blaze like a tree?

In a world always late afternoon,
In the circular smells of a slow wind,
I listen to the weeds' vesperal whine,
Longing for absolutes that never come.
And shapes make me afraid:
The dance of natural objects in the mind,
The immediate sheen, the reality of straw,
The shadows crawling down a sunny wall.

　　A bird sings out in solitariness
　　A thin harsh song. The day dies in a child.
　　How close we are to the sad animals!
　　I need a pool; I need a puddle's calm.

O my bones,
Beware those perpetual beginnings,
Thinning the soul's substance;
The swan's dread of the darkening shore,

Or these insects pulsing near my skin,
The songs from a spiral tree.

> Fury of wind, and no apparent wind,
> A gust blowing the leaves suddenly upward,
> A vine lashing in dry fury,
> A man chasing a cat,
> With a broken umbrella,
> Crying softly.

2

It is difficult to say all things are well,
When the worst is about to arrive;
It is fatal to woo yourself,
However graceful the posture.

> Loved heart, what can I say?
> When I was a lark, I sang;
> When I was a worm, I devoured.

> The self says, I am;
> The heart says, I am less;
> The spirit says, you are nothing.

Mist alters the rocks. What can I tell my bones?
My desire's a wind trapped in a cave.
The spirit declares itself to these rocks.
I'm a small stone, loose in the shale.
Love is my wound.

The wide streams go their way,
The pond lapses back into a glassy silence.
The cause of God in me—has it gone?

Do these bones live? Can I live with these bones?
Mother, mother of us all, tell me where I am!
O to be delivered from the rational into the realm of pure song,
My face on fire, close to the points of a star,
A learned nimble girl,
Not drearily bewitched,
But sweetly daft.

To try to become like God
Is far from becoming God.
O, but I seek and care!

I rock in my own dark,
Thinking, God has need of me.
The dead love the unborn.

3

Weeds turn toward the wind weed-skeletons.
How slowly all things alter.
Existence dares perpetuate a soul,
A wedge of heaven's light, autumnal song.
I hear a beat of birds, the plangent wings
That disappear into a waning moon;
The barest speech of light among the stones.

To what more vast permission have I come?
When I walk past a vat, water joggles.
I no longer cry for green in the midst of cinders,
Or dream of the dead, and their holes.
Mercy has many arms.

Instead of a devil with horns, I prefer a serpent with scales;
In temptation, I rarely seek counsel;

A prisoner of smells, I would rather eat than pray.
I'm released from the dreary dance of opposites.
The wind rocks with my wish; the rain shields me;
I live in light's extreme; I stretch in all directions;
Sometimes I think I'm several.

The sun! The sun! And all we can become!
And the time ripe for running to the moon!
In the long fields, I leave my father's eye;
And shake the secrets from my deepest bones;
My spirit rises with the rising wind;
I'm thick with leaves and tender as a dove,
I take the liberties a short life permits—
I seek my own meekness;
I recover my tenderness by long looking.
By midnight I love everything alive.
Who took the darkness from the air?
I'm wet with another life.
Yea, I have gone and stayed.

What came to me vaguely is now clear,
As if released by a spirit,
Or agency outside me.
Unprayed-for,
And final.

B-30